A CRITICAL ANSWER

TO

Michael Sproul's

God's Word Preserved

D. A. WAITE, Th.D., Ph.D.

275 of Sproul's Statements Analyzed Carefully for Errors, Misrepresentations, and Serious Falsehoods

Published by
THE BIBLE FOR TODAY PRESS
900 Park Avenue
Collingswood, New Jersey 08108
U.S.A.

Church Phone: 856-854-4747
BFT Phone: 856-854-4452
Orders: 1-800-John 10:9
e-mail: BFT@BibleForToday.org
Website: www.BibleForToday.org
fax: 856-854-2464

We Use and Defend
the King James Bible

April, 2008
BFT3308

Copyright, 2008
All Rights Reserved

ISBN 978-56848-058-9

Acknowledgments

I wish to acknowledge the assistance of the following people:

- **Dianne W. Cosby**--our daughter, for listening carefully to these radio messages that were broadcast by radio and by the Internet around the world; for typing these messages accurately from the cassette tapes; and for putting them into computer format to be used as the basis for this book;

- **Yvonne Sanborn Waite**--my wife, for encouraging the publication of these radio messages; for reading the manuscript carefully; and for giving helpful suggestions for the body of the book and for the cover.

- **Loretta Smith**--a friend and former attender at our church, for reading the book carefully; for giving needed corrections; and for making the writing as clear as possible.

- **Daniel S. Waite**--the Assistant to the Bible For Today Director, for keeping my computer working properly; and for checking the proofs when ready.

FOREWORD

• *A Critical Answer to God's Word Preserved*, is important because it is an answer to a current book written by a Fundamentalist Baptist Pastor of the Tri-City Baptist Church. His name is Dr. Michael Sproul who is also the chairman of the board of the International Baptist College in Tempe, Arizona.

• In addition to Sproul's Fundamentalist Baptist background, he is an officer in the Fundamental Baptist Fellowship (FBF) whose leaders are either graduates of Bob Jones University (BJU) or else loyal to the BJU position on the Bible issues. Sproul has joined the BJU position in two areas: (1) disbelief in the preservation of the original Hebrew, Aramaic, and Greek Words, and (2) a strong opposition to those who maintain this position.

• In this book, I have quoted and given comments on 275 of Sproul's **STATEMENTS**. Though I have seen a brief refutation of Sproul's book, I do not know of a thorough treatment. For this reason, I believe it is important to counteract some of the many falsehoods in Sproul's book more extensively. I hope those on both sides of the Bible Version debate will read this book in order to examine the many inaccuracies, misunderstandings, and downright lies contained in Sproul's book.

• The reader is encouraged to get two of my recent books answering the BJU arguments on Bible versions and Bible preservation: (1) *Fundamentalist Deception on Bible Preservation* **(BFT #3234 @ $8.00 + $4.00 S&H)**. (2) *Bob Jones University's Errors on Bible Preservation* **(BFT #3259 @ $8.00 + $4.00 S&H)**. May the Lord give you discernment in this current battle for our Bible.

Sincerely yours for God's Words,

D. a. Waite

Pastor D. A. Waite, Th.D., Ph.D.
Director, The Bible For Today, Incorporated

Table of Contents

A CRITICAL

ANSWER

TO

Michael Sproul's

God's Word Preserved

Introductory Considerations

This book is an attempt to bring a partial answer and reply to a number of errors and false statements in a book entitled *God's Word Preserved: A Defense of Historic Separatist Definitions and Beliefs*. It is a large book of 403 pages. The author is Dr. Michael Sproul. He graduated from Calvary Baptist Seminary in Lansdale, Pennsylvania. He is both the pastor of the Tri-State Baptist Church, and the chairman of the board of the International Baptist College. Both of these organizations are located in Tempe, Arizona.

Since there are many references in this book to *THE FUNDAMENTALS*, I have checked on these quotations from *THE FUNDAMENTALS: A Testimony to the Truth*, printed in 1915. This can be seen on many websites. This is one URL: **http://www.xmission.com/~fidelis/**

Though there are many false and misleading statements in Sproul's book, I will be limiting my comments to only 275 of the most egregious statements. This material was first given on a series of my radio broadcasts.

275 Statements And My Comments
PREFACE
(pp. 11-17)

God's "Word" Not "Words"

STATEMENT #1. The full title of this book is: *GOD'S WORD PRESERVED--A Defense of Historic Separatist Definitions and Beliefs* (front cover).

COMMENT #1. By the use of the term, "*God's Word,*" Sproul does not mean the preservation of all the original Hebrew, Aramaic and Greek Words of God. As many of his contemporary Fundamentalist friends, by "Word" he means only the "*ideas, thoughts, concepts, message, truth, or teachings,*" but not "*Words.*"

Using KJB But Fighting It

STATEMENT #2. (p. 13) "*From the outset let me make it perfectly clear that I love my Old Scofield King James Version. I preach out of it every Sunday.*"

COMMENT #2. When people say that they love their old King James Bible whether it is an *Old Scofield King James Version,* or something else, be careful. I really love the King James Bible, but I also stand for it and defend it. He **claims** he loves it, but he does not defend it. In fact, he pokes holes in both the King James Bible and the original Hebrew, Aramaic, and Greek Words that underlie it.

Using TR But Fighting It

STATEMENT #3. (p. 14) "*I write from the perspective of a preference for the Byzantine Majority Text. My purpose is not to defend that position necessarily, but I am certain some of my beliefs will be apparent. I preach every week from the Old Scofield King James Bible, a version that relies on Blayney's 1769 revision. . . . International Baptist College . . . currently uses the 1894 Textus Receptus of Scrivener in the classroom and our academy only uses Blayney's* *revision."*

COMMENT #3. What he is saying there is they use the text and Words of the New Testament from Scrivener's Textus Receptus that underlies our King James Bible. He says that basically he defends only the Byzantine Majority Text, which changes those Textus Receptus Greek Words in about 1800 places. I am glad he does not agree with the Westcott/Hort or Nestle/Aland or United Bible Societies Critical Texts. By the time he finishes his various condemnations in his book, you will wonder what he really does believe. I am glad he uses the King James Bible and preaches from it every Sunday. I am glad his college currently uses Scrivener's Textus Receptus Greek text. I hope they continue to use it. I am glad his academy uses Blayney's King James Bible Revision. I hope they keep it. However, to have it and use it, but undermine it is somewhat hypocritical.

We Have "Inerrant" Greek Words

STATEMENT #4. (p. 14) *"However, I do not believe either Blayney's Revision or Scrivener's printed Greek Text is inerrant."*

COMMENT #4. I do not use the term "inerrant" for the King James Bible. That does not mean I believe it to be "errant," however. I do not think it has any *"translational"* errors, but I do not use the word *"inerrant"* or *"infallible."* I do use those words for the Hebrew, Aramaic, and Greek Words which underlie the King James Bible. Sproul does not hold to my position on Scrivener's Greek text. If so, why does he use it in his college? If he has some questions about the King James Bible, why does he preach from it each week and why does his academy use it? Again, this is somewhat hypocritical.

No "Inspired" Apostles & Prophets

STATEMENT #5. (p. 14) *"However, I do believe that both Scrivener's Greek Text and Blayney's Revision of the King James are good and faithful to the original writings of the apostles and prophets __whom the Holy Spirit inspired__."*

COMMENT #5. Sproul does not refer to the *"original writings"* that were *"inspired,"* but the "apostles and prophets __whom the Holy Spirit inspired.__"

> The Holy Spirit did not *"inspire"* any men. He did not *"inspire"* apostles. He did not *"inspire"* prophets.

This is a serious theological heresy by Sproul. The doctrine of inspiration is found only in 2 Timothy 3:16 with the words, *"All scripture is given by inspiration of God."* The five words, *"given by inspiration of God"* is the translation of the word THEOPNEUSTOS. It means literally, *"God breathed."*

The words for *"all scripture"* are PASA GRAPHE which refers to all that has been written down. God breathed out the Words of the apostles and prophets, not the apostles and prophets themselves.

Even one of Sproul's *"Fundamentalist Fathers,"* James M. Gray, in Chapter 20 of *The Fundamentals*, in Gray's article "The Inspiration of the Bible-- Definition, Extent and Proof," wrote:

> *"4. When we speak of the Holy Spirit coming upon the men in order to complete the composition of the books, it should be further understood that **the object is not the inspiration of the men but the books — not the writers but the writings.** It terminates upon the record, in other words, and not upon the human instrument who made it."*

Gray clearly contradicts Sproul's error on *"inspired writers."*

"Inerrancy" Was Before 1950

STATEMENT 6. (p. 14) *"However, inscribing inerrancy to either the English translation of 1611 and/or any of its revisions or to Scrivener's 1894 Greek text or to any TR previous to Scrivener is an unknown position for any mainstream Evangelical or Fundamentalist leader who lived before 1950."*

COMMENT #6. I believe that the Words in Scrivener's Greek text are the original Greek Words of the New Testament that have been preserved for us. As such, they are inspired or God-breathed Words--infallible Words, inerrant Words, and perfect Words. I do not believe that the King James Bible's words were God-breathed or inspired of God. They were translated from God's preserved, inspired, inerrant, and perfect Words.

STATEMENT #7. (p. 14) *"The first appearance of the title Textus Receptus (Received Text) occurred, for promotional purposes, not as a statement of doctrinal orthodoxy."*

COMMENT #7. In 1633, the Elziver edition of the Greek New Testament stated in Latin that these Greek Words was a *"text received by all."* The Latin words in question were: *"**Textum** ergo habes, nunc ab omnibus **receptum**, in quo nihil immutatum aut corruptum damus."* The Elziver brothers were merely saying that *"Therefore we have a **text**, now **received** by all, in which is nothing changed or corrupted."* **In other words this was a text that had been passed down from apostolic times, and that is when the expression first appeared.** Dr. Sproul implies that this was the first time the Textus Receptus or the Received Text first came into existence. It is certainly recognized that though this was the time when this name was give to it in 1633, it certainly was not the time that this text began. It is clear that this *"text"* had been *"received"* by all for hundreds of years past. The *"text"* originated with Paul, Peter, James and all the other authors of our Greek New

Testament.

No "Inerrant" Fundamental Fathers

STATEMENT #8. (p. 15) *"Whatever textual position the heirs of our Fundamental Fathers might adopt, their belief system should never involve denigrating or attacking the Fathers who gave them life and breath."*

    COMMENT #8. If the Fathers of the fundamentalist movement were wrong, we must expose, attack, and seek to correct their wrong understandings, beliefs, theology, and doctrines. We must defend and contend for the Scriptures, especially when Fundamentalists have misinterpreted them.

    "Beloved, when I gave all diligence to write unto you of the common salvation, it was needful for me to write unto you, and exhort *you* that <u>ye should earnestly contend for the faith which was once delivered unto the saints</u>." (Jude 1:3b)

"*The faith*" mentioned in this verse refers to the body of doctrine found in the Bible.

No "Misquoting"

STATEMENT #9. (p. 14) *"The Holy Spirit does not need the craftiness of men's reasoning either in misquoting or omitting vital information for His Truth to be vindicated. Directly citing a source's intent and accurately explaining the position of an individual with whom one disagrees is vital in a Christian discussion."*

    COMMENT #9. That is what I seek to do in our **Bible For Today of the Air Weekly Radio Broadcasts** in defending our King James Bible. These broadcasts are the basis of this present book. I never seek to misquote any of our opponents, and I will not seek to misquote Dr. Michael Sproul in his book, *God's Word Preserved--A Defense of Historic Separatist Definitions and Beliefs.* I want to quote him exactly as I have done throughout the ministry of my radio programs and throughout our other **Bible For Today** ministries.

"Inerrancy" Not in Originals Only

STATEMENT #10. (p. 15, footnote 7) *"As the reader will better understand after reading Chapter Four, the position of 'inerrancy only in the original writings with the modern Christian having accurate language copies' was a position of John Gill, ... "*

    COMMENT #10. I believe John Gill believed that those language copies were not only "*accurate*," but also "*inerrant*" copies of those original writings. God promised to preserve His Hebrew, Aramaic, and Greek

Words inerrantly, and He did preserve them. That is our belief. Some of our fundamentalist brethren do not believe that. They do not believe that God's original Hebrew, Aramaic, and Greek Words have been preserved inerrantly, but I do.

Books Against Sproul's Views

STATEMENT #11. (p. 16) *"I write, not eagerly, but out of a broken spirit for my people who are receiving unsolicited videos and books that **attack** the leadership of our church and its heritage."*

COMMENT #11. When somebody in his church is wrong their error should be *"attacked,"* not the person. When Michael Sproul is wrong, his position should be *"attacked,"* not him personally. That is what we seek to do in our Bible For Today ministry. We are sorry that he brings in people who do not have the proper position.

"Ruckmanism" & "KJV-Only"

STATEMENT #12. (p. 16) *"They sense the dangers of starting down the slippery slop to Ruckmanism, which they perceive is the direction of the 'KJV-only' movement. They are concerned about the dogmatism and the spirit of many Christians who are involved in that movement."*

COMMENT #12. In the first place, my position on the King James Bible and the Greek, Aramaic, and Hebrew Words that underlie it is not a Ruckmanite position at all. He is saying that the people of the *"KJV-only"* movement lean toward the Ruckmanism. That is why I do not like the term "King James only." That term puts into the same corner all of the Ruckman positions as well as the positions, which are sane and sensible. I do not use that term *"KJV-only."* I only use the King James Bible in preaching and study. I reject the libelous term *"KJV-only"* that is applied to the Ruckman position with which I strongly disagree.

"Word" Preservation Only

STATEMENT #13. (p. 16) He writes about *"the accurate preservation of the Word of God without adopting an extreme position that misrepresents history and misrepresents biblical passages."*

COMMENT #13. Notice he does not talk about the preservation of the *"Words"* of God simple the *"Word"* of God. Like his Bob Jones University counterparts, whom I have analyzed on the radio and in booklets answering their materials, they use the term *"Word"* of God instead of *"Words"* of God. *"Word"* of God to them simply means only the *"ideas, thoughts, concepts, message, truth, or teachings"* of God, but not the actual *"Words"* of God. I believe that Sproul is using the same terminology here. Since the average

Christian today equates the "Word" of God with the "Words" of God, by Sproul's book title, *God's Word Preserved*, he has greatly deceived his readers into thinking that he believes something that he, in fact, denies.

Afraid of "Videos" & "Books"

STATEMENT #14. (p. 17) *"However, uninvited videos and books attacking Separatism's historic position, which reflects the beliefs of our church's leadership for over thirty years, have regularly invaded my sheepfold."*

COMMENT #14. He doesn't like anybody giving his church members, or having them buy for themselves, videos or books that do not reflect his position. Everybody has a right to listen to and to read what they want to listen to and to read. If they need truth and they don't have it in their own church, there is no good reason why they should not be supplied with it.

INTRODUCTION
(pp. 19-24)

"Fathers" Rather Than the Bible

STATEMENT #15. (p. 21) *"The various 'KJV-Only' views are discussed, and only to illustrate their departure from the biblically and historically accurate definitions and beliefs of the Separatist Fathers."*

COMMENT #15. Sproul's problem is that some people disagree with the *"beliefs of the Separatist Fathers"* rather than with the Bible. This is a very weak position.

Dr. David Otis Fuller's 1970 Book

STATEMENT #16. (p. 21) *"For twenty years I have read the discussion of versions and texts. . . . However, with the advent of David Otis Fuller's book, <u>Which Bible</u> in 1970, my generation began the discussion that today affects Baptists when they move to a new city and begin searching for a church home."*

COMMENT #16. That is true. Dr. David Otis Fuller's Book, *Which Bible*, influenced me and got me and many others on the right track. I was taught at Dallas Theological Seminary from the Westcott and Hort Greek Text. That is the exact text they sold us at the bookstore. I did not know there was another Greek text until I read Dr. Fuller's book. He was quoting and condensing Dean John W. Burgon's excellent books which **the Dean Burgon Society has now reprinted.**

KJB Position & Attending Church

STATEMENT #17. (p. 21) He is talking about when he visits his first time attendees. They often ask him: *"'What do you believe about the King James Version'? Unfortunately, for better or worse, the issue of versions for many people is now <u>the</u> only doctrinal reason for joining or leaving a church."*

COMMENT #17. What's wrong with asking about what version you use? I would not like to go to a church that does not use and defend the King James Bible. I have not gone to a church that uses some other version than the King James Version. Why should I? This is important. When people ask me where they should go to church in a particular area, I tell them to check the yellow pages and call the pastor on the phone and ask him what version he uses and what he believes about the Scriptures. Why go to a church whose Greek text that underlies their New Testament is different in 8,000 places from the Greek text that underlies the King James Bible? Why go to a church that has 356 doctrinal passages that have false doctrine in them because the wrong Greek text was used? Why go to a church that uses a Greek New Testament that drops out 2,886 Greek words from the Traditional Text such as the NIV, NASV, ASV, RSV, NRSV, ESV and other modern versions do?

Attacking Positions, Not People

STATEMENT #18. (pp. 21-22) *"When I refer to KJV-only, I am not exclusively referring to a theological position; but I am also referring to a spirit. KJV-onlyism is much like new Evangelicalism in that it is a spirit or mood. It is a spirit that believes that it must separate from or attack other brothers in Christ for their choices on the issue of text and translations."*

COMMENT #18. I don't attack the *"brothers in Christ"* personally. I attack the unbiblical theology and the unbiblical beliefs that these *"brothers in Christ"* wrongly hold to. I'm not attacking this man, Michael Sproul, but I am attacking some of his beliefs and positions he holds to in this book. That's what it means to *"earnestly **contend for the faith** which was once delivered unto the saints"* (Jude 3).

Sproul's False Use of "KJV-only"

STATEMENT #19. (p. 22) *"I'm not using 'KJV-only' as a pejorative or degrading description of one who has a strong preference for Blayney's 1769 revision and loves it, yet, who can fellowship with other Fundamentalists who may not prefer that revision as strongly."*

COMMENT #19. Now he makes a distinction between those who use the King James and believe in it and those who don't believe in it as strongly. He wants you to break down any fence you might have as far as cooperation between those who use and prefer other versions and perversions. He does not want you or your church to stand exclusively for the use and defense of the King James Bible. He can say he preaches out of an Old Scofield King James all he wants, but if he has a church that is filled with modern versions that pervert the Bible in many areas, it shows his lack of serious stand for that Bible. Why does he preach from a Bible he lacks confidence in and which he trashes in his book in many areas? I believe he is being hypocritical in this.

Separation Because of the Bible

STATEMENT #20. (p. 23) *"I have friends on all sides of this issue, and I am determined not to separate from them."*

COMMENT #20. The Bible says, *"Can two walk together, except they be agreed?"* (Amos 3:3). If we disagree on the most important thing in the world, the Bible, how can we continue to *"walk together"*? I am not comfortable going to a church that is not unified on the King James Bible because I am strongly convinced that it is the only accurate English Bible. I have outlined this in my book, *Defending the King James Bible*. Those using other versions led by Bob Jones University (BJU) and other schools who follow their lead are separating from us who stand for the King James Bible and its underlying Hebrew, Aramaic, and Greek Words.

FBF's Separation Due to the Bible

The recent resolution by the Fundamental Baptist Fellowship (with strong BJU leadership) is an example of this, calling us *"schismatic 'brethren'"* (*"heretics"* in the KJB in Titus 3:10). In that term, they not only call fellow-Fundamentalists *"heretics"* but doubt that they are genuine *"brethren"* by putting the word in quotation marks. Here is a copy:

RESOLUTIONS FROM THE 81st ANNUAL MEETING OF THE FUNDAMENTAL BAPTIST FELLOWSHIP!
RESOLUTION #01.5 REGARDING
SCHISMATIC "BRETHREN"
OCTOBER 3, 2001

"In light of the public attacks and false accusations upon the FBF, its leaders, and other like-minded Fundamentalist institutions regarding their respective positions on the text of Scripture and translations, we reaffirm that within the historic orthodox doctrine of Bibliology these are matters of soul-liberty and should not be a test of fellowship for Fundamentalists. Since not all professors or pastors have expertise in the field of textual studies, disagreements regarding text or translation should be resolved by honest discussion as opposed to libelous contention. Those who repeatedly attempt to unnecessarily divide Fundamentalists over this issue and refuse to repent should be regarded as schismatics who must be rejected as the Word of God instructs (Romans 16:17-18; Titus 3:9-11; 1 Corinthians 3:10-17)."

That resolution is saying that if those who defend the King James Bible and the Hebrew, Aramaic, and Greek Words which underlie it, and do not repent of that position, they are to be counted as *"schismatics"* or *"heretics."* If such *"repentance"* does not occur, there should even be a doubt that they are genuine Christian *"brethren."* Why should I *"repent"* from something that I have no problem with, and agree with, which is a true Biblical position? I'm not going to *"repent"* of truth.

"Little or No Training" Opponents?

STATEMENT #21. (p. 24) *"Amazingly many people who have little* *or no training in these matters 'dogmatize' quickly on this subject."*

COMMENT #21. I take great offense at Sproul's belittling the *"training"* of those who disagree with him. He says that people who *"have little or no training in these matters 'dogmatize.'"* I *"dogmatize"* in this area, but I did not do so *"quickly."* I have been studying, speaking about, and writing on this subject since 1970. I believe firmly in what I am saying. I wonder if he is sure about what he believes. If you believe something strongly you should shout it out. I don't know whether or not Michael Sproul has *"little or no training in these matters,"* but (without wanting to brag, but solely for the purpose of documentation and setting the record straight) here is a quotation of a summary of this writer's *"little or no training in these matters"*:

> *"The writer was thoroughly prepared and trained in the original biblical languages of Hebrew and Greek. He received credit in these languages either at the University of Michigan (1945-48, Classical Greek) or at the Dallas Theological Seminary (1948-53, N.T. Greek) as follows: In Greek, 66 semester hours; in Hebrew, 25 semester hours; a total of 91 semester hours in combined biblical languages.*
>
> *In addition to these 91 semester hours, the author has received credit for 27 additional hours in other foreign languages, divided as follows: Latin, 8 semester hours; French, 8 semester hours; Spanish, 11 semester hours. The grand total of foreign languages in terms of semester hours, in addition to the many other related courses taken at schools for work on the author's A.B., M.A., Th.M., Th.D., and/or Ph.D., has been 118 semester hours in foreign languages. This is only 2 semester hours short of a solid 4-year undergraduate course consisting of 120 semester hours required for graduation in most universities today.*
>
> *Four of the five-residency-earned degrees mentioned above (M.A., Th.M., Th.D., and Ph.D.) required research theses and/or dissertations which prepared him to deal satisfactorily with documentation and evidence. Whatever other differences the modern critics of the King James Bible and its underlying Hebrew and Greek texts might have with this writer, they cannot justifiably criticize his preparations and training in these essential disciplines."* [*The Case for the King James Bible*, by Pastor D. A. Waite, Th.D., Ph.D. p. 2, available as **BFT #83** @ **$7.00 + $4.00 S&H**].

STATEMENT #22. (p. 24) *"After about twenty years and literally thousands of hours of study, I am aware of the fact there are many things I do not know."*

COMMENT #22. I would agree with that. I have spent since 1970 (more years than he has) studying this subject, and there are things that I do not know either. That is a statement we can agree on.

CHAPTER ONE:
MAN'S PROBLEMS WITH
GOD'S METHOD OF
COMMUNICATION
(pp. 25-50)

Misuse of the "KJV-Only" Term

STATEMENT #23. (p. 25) This page begins his Chapter 1 *"Man's Problems with God's Method of Communication" – Theological Movements of the Late 19th and Early 20th Century and Defining 'KJV-Only' Views."*

COMMENT #23. As I have said before many times, I do not go along with that *"KJV-Only"* term. It is a slanderous smear-term that is pronounced not only against the followers of Peter Ruckman, but also against those of us who have a healthy stance on the King James Bible and its underlying Hebrew, Aramaic, and Greek Words. In contrast to the Ruckmanites, we do not believe the King James Bible has been *"given by inspiration of God,"* *"inspired by God,"* *"God-breathed,"* or *"inspired"* as many Ruckmanites do. We believe that the King James Bible is a translation from the preserved Hebrew, Aramaic and Greek Words that underlie it. We believe those Hebrew, Aramaic, and Greek Words are copies of the originals and are therefore preserved, inspired, infallible, and inerrant Words. That is where we put our inerrancy. We do not like this *"King James Only"* term that mixes our proper and sound views with the improper and unsound views of Dr. Peter Ruckman and his followers who teach that the King James Bible is a special *"revelation"* and therefore can correct the Hebrew, Aramaic, and Greek Words that underlie it. This is pure heresy with which I justifiably do not want to be identified in any way.

"Inspiration" Is For Originals Only

STATEMENT #24. (p. 25) Sproul quotes John Gill, *"Inspiration is to be understood of the Scriptures, as in the original languages in which they were written, and not a translation."*

COMMENT #24. I agree with John Gill's quotation about *"inspiration."* This is why I reject Sproul's slanderous term, *"KJV-Only."* Translations, no matter if they are in French, German, Spanish or English, or in any other language, must never be termed *"God-breathed," "inspired by God,"* or *"inspired"* in any way. These terms must be used only for the originals and accurate copies of the Hebrew, Aramaic, and Greek Words used by God to compose our Bible.

Exalting "Fundamentalist Fathers"

STATEMENT #25. (p. 28) *"Into this theological breach of modernists rode a group of courageous men. Today we call them the Fundamentalist Fathers."*

COMMENT #25. Pastor Sproul is exalting the *"Fundamentalist Fathers"* as if they were perfect in all that they wrote in 1915 in their ninety chapters called *The Fundamentals: A Testimony to the Truth.* At first, this work came out in twelve volumes. Later it was published in four volumes. It is now available online at **http://www.xmission.com/~fidelis/** Sproul elevates these fallible men to the status of apostles, prophets, or even to the very Words of God Himself. If these *"Fathers"* have some imperfect doctrines or teachings, they should be corrected, not canonized. We should inspect their views carefully. Sproul acts as if anyone departs from the things from the *"Fundamentalist Fathers"* as found in *The Fundamentals*, he is departing from the truth. I do not buy that at all. Truth did not end in 1915. The understanding of the Bible did not stop in 1915. Some of the defects, shortcomings, and errors of these *"Fundamentalist Fathers"* as found in *"The Fundamentals"* will be cited later in this analysis.

Book Is Wrong on Bible Preservation

STATEMENT #26. (p. 29) On footnote #13, Sproul wrote: *"James B. Williams and Randolf Shaylor, God's Word in our Hands: The Bible Preserved for Us . . . This is an excellent history on Fundamentalism as it is applied to the 'KJV-only' controversy."*

COMMENT #26. That book is not an *"excellent history"* on anything. It is a plea for Bible-believing Christians to change their definition of Bible preservation from the preservation of the **"***Words***"** of God to merely the preservation of the **"***Word***"** of God. For them, the **"***Word***"** means only the **"***ideas, thoughts, concepts, message, truth, or teachings***,"** but not the **"***Words***."** I have answered this book, some of whose writers are connected to Bob Jones University as BJU graduates or in other ways. I call it *Fundamentalist Deception on Bible Preservation.* It can be ordered as BFT #3234 @ $8.00 + $4.00 S&H.

"More" vs. "Less" Educated"?

STATEMENT #27. (p. 31) *"It is important for separatists to remember that God has used both the educated and less educated in His service. Some of the arguments that swirl around the issue of the preservation of the KJV are really the fruit of a deeper tension among separatists. That tension is the one that exists between the more educated and less educated wings of Fundamentalism. Both sides have at times been guilty of derogatory remarks concerning the other 'camp.' Neither should have the attitude that they are more spiritual, either because they are educated, or because they are not educated."*

COMMENT #27. This battle is not between the educated and the uneducated. Sproul is trying to say that he is a big educated man with his various degrees that he holds. His degrees are listed in the book on page 354. He mentions these degrees, as if to say he is on the side of the educated, and the other people whom he names, like myself, who stand for and defend the King James Bible and the Words underlying it, are ignorant and should stay out of this argument. Sproul says he has the following degrees: a Bachelor of Arts (B.A.), a Master of Divinity (M.DIV.), and a Doctorate of Ministry (D. Min.). Those are his degrees. I suppose he thinks that he is among the "*educated.*" When Sproul says that, *"That tension is the one that exists between the **more educated** and **less educated** wings of Fundamentalism,"* he is saying that his critical text-onlyism side is the educated side and the people who are on the side of the King James Bible and the Hebrew, Aramaic, and Greek Words that underlie it are uneducated. We have plenty of men on our side of the battle who are educated in the things of the Scriptures and the languages of the Bible.

I will repeat here what I quoted earlier in this analysis concerning my own education and training whom Sproul, I am sure, is putting on the side of the "*less educated wings of Fundamentalism.*"

"*This writer* [Dr. D. A. Waite] *was thoroughly prepared and trained in the original biblical languages of Hebrew and Greek. He received credit in these languages either at the University of Michigan (1945-48, Classical Greek) or at the Dallas Theological Seminary (1948-53, Biblical Greek & Hebrew) as follows: In Greek, 66 semester hours; in Hebrew, 25 semester hours; **a total of 91 semester hours in combined biblical languages**.*

*In addition to these 91 semester hours, the author has received credit for 27 additional hours in other foreign languages, divided as follows: Latin, 8 semester hours; French, 8 semester hours; Spanish, 11 semester hours. The **grand total of foreign languages in terms of semester hours**, in addition to the many other related courses taken at schools for work on the author's A.B., M.A., Th.M., Th.D., and/or*

*Ph.D., **has been 118 semester hours in foreign languages**. This is only 2 semester hours short of a solid 4-year undergraduate course consisting of 120 semester hours required for graduation in most universities today.*

Four of the five-residency-earned degrees mentioned above (M.A., Th.M., Th.D., and Ph.D.) required research theses and/or dissertations which prepared him to deal satisfactorily with documentation and evidence. Whatever other differences the modern critics of the King James Bible and its underlying Hebrew and Greek texts might have with this writer, they cannot justifiably criticize his preparations and training in these essential disciplines." [*The Case for the King James Bible*, by Pastor D. A. Waite, Th.D., Ph.D. p. 2, available as **BFT #83** @ $7.00 + $4.00 S&H]

KJB Not a "Perfect Rock" Now?

STATEMENT #28. (p. 33) *"The Word of God has stood the test and the most well recognized version in American culture is the King James Version of the Bible. It is readily apparent how some can believe in the version 'we have always used' as a perfect rock in a turbulent era."*

COMMENT #28. Sproul said that the King James Bible is *"the most well recognized version in American culture."* As the *"Word of God,"* he implies that it has *"stood the test of time."* But he does not think it is a *"perfect rock in a turbulent era."* If he doesn't believe the King James Bible is a *"rock,"* why does he preach from it in his church every Sunday and in the mid-week service? Why doesn't he use some other version? This is sheer hypocrisy on Sproul's part! He is a friend with everybody and his brother who use different kinds of Bible versions and perversions. He wants everybody to be friendly and to not have a firm position as far as what the real Bible is. The same is true of the differences in Hebrew, Aramaic, and Greek Words that underlie the various versions of the Bible. He does not want to have a strong and distinctive position on the Bible issue. Beware of those who claim to use and love the King James Bible, yet tear it apart in various ways in their life, writing, and ministry.

"Fathers of Fundamentalism" Beliefs

STATEMENT #29. (p. 33) *"Yet, one must ask, did the **Fathers of Fundamentalism**, when faced with attacks against the Word try to escape the complexities of the arguments surrounding the accuracy and preservation of God's Word by running to a 'KJV-only' position as some currant separatists have done?"*

COMMENT #29. How does what the *"Fathers of Fundamentalism"* may have done pertain to Biblical truth today? In 1915 they did not have all the facts about the various issues that we have today. They had not debated it and gone back and forth and written books on it and studied it out.

Dean John W. Burgon published his book, *The Revision Revised*, in 1883. 1915 was only 32 years after that book by Dean Burgon and men of that caliber had been written. They had not digested all of these facts. The *"Fathers of Fundamentalism"* are considered by Sproul to be inerrant in their pronouncements in their volumes called *The Fundamentals*. That is what Sproul is trying to push. That is why Sproul has a sub-title, *"In Defense of Historic Separatist Definitions and Beliefs."* He is treating these Fundamentalist writers like the Roman Catholic Church considers the proclamations of the Pope of Rome. Sproul is repeatedly saying that if those *Fathers of Fundamentalism* believed something back in 1915, or did not believe something in 1915, we of today should never question any of their decisions. They should be unquestionably accepted, not because they are Biblical, but because of their 1915 beliefs of *"Historic Separatists."* This is a serious and fatal error. Sproul has repeated throughout his book.

Consider just a few *"beliefs"* of some of these *"Fathers of Fundamentalism"* as found in *The Fundamentals* of 1915:

- 1. Thomas Spurgeon, in Chapter 45 entitled *"Salvation by Grace,"* wrote that *"the salvation and the faith are both the gift Of God."* In this, he misinterprets Ephesians 2:8-10. In this chapter, he reveals his five point **hyper-Calvinism** which, I strongly believe, is unscriptural. Does Sproul believe we have no right to disagree with this position?
- 2. In Chapter 85, Professor Charles R. Erdman wrote on the theme of *"The Coming of Christ,"* under the section, *"3. IMMINENT,"* he wrote about *"inspired writers"* of the Bible. This is the same **heresy** that Sproul believes and that I dispute strongly. Does Sproul believe we nave no right to disagree with this position?
- 3. In Chapter 85, Professor Charles R. Erdman, under the section, *"2. HIS COMING, GLORIOUS,"* speaks only of the Lord Jesus Christ's second coming to the earth in glory, but never includes (and therefore denies) **the Lord's coming in the air to rapture the saved ones to Heaven before the Tribulation.** Does Sproul believe we nave no right to disagree with this position?

Do you see the danger of Sproul's exaltation of a group of human beings as being more authoritative than the clear teachings of the Bible itself?

STATEMENT #30. (pp. 33-34) *"Yet over the last thirty or forty years, a growing group of conservative Bible believers have rejected their Fundamentalist Fathers' position on preservation and have demanded an emphasis on the perfection of the 1611 or the 1769 KJV, the Greek Textus Receptus (TR), the Hebrew Masoretic Text (MT), or some type of synthesis among the scores of TRs and MTs in existence."*

COMMENT #30. Sproul again recommends the worship of the *"Fundamentalist Fathers."* He says that we have rejected the *"Fundamentalist Fathers' position."* This is serious heresy. It is false teaching that all truth was frozen with the publication of *The Fundamentals* in 1915.

> As I have said many times, I do not believe that *"perfection"* is in any translation of the Bible, but rather in the Hebrew, Aramaic, and Greek Words underlying the King James Bible. Perfection lies with the Words that the Lord gave to mankind. *"As for God, His way is perfect . . ."* (Psalm 18:30a)

If I were to say, as the followers of Peter Ruckman do, that the King James Bible were *"perfect,"* how would I explain the presence of the unscriptural Apocrypha contained in it? I believe the King James Bible is the most accurate English translation in existence from the proper underlying Hebrew, Aramaic, and Greek Words.

As for the *"preservation"* of the Hebrew, Aramaic, and Greek Words of the original writings, let me say the following. I believe that the Lord Jesus Christ made it crystal clear that His Words would be preserved. John 16:12-14 makes it clear that the Lord Jesus Christ is the Source of all of the Greek Words. By extension, it is true for the Old Testament Hebrew and Aramaic Words:

> *"[12] I have yet many things to say unto you, but ye cannot bear them now. [13] Howbeit when he, the Spirit of truth, is come, he will guide you into all truth: for he shall not speak of* [or FROM] *himself; but whatsoever he shall hear, that shall he speak: and he will shew you things to come. [14] He shall glorify me: for he shall receive of mine, and shall shew it unto you."*

> The Lord Jesus Christ said: *"Heaven and earth shall pass away, but my Words shall not pass away"* (Matthew 24:35; Mark 13:31; and Luke 21:33). The Greek term for *"not"* is OU ME. This is the strongest Greek negative particle in the language. It means *"never, never."* This is an unmistakable promise of the *"preservation"* of the Bible's Hebrew, Aramaic, and Greek Words. I believe the Scriptures and the Lord Jesus Christ's promises.

If some or all of the *"Fundamentalist Fathers"* might have had a different position on Bible *"preservation"* why should this be taken as truth beyond all question?

One of Sproul's *"Fundamentalist Fathers,"* James M. Gray, in Chapter 20 of *The Fundamentals*, under *"Argument for Words,"* wrote:

> *"In the third place, Christ teaches that the scriptures are inspired as to their words. In the Sermon on the Mount He said, 'Think not that I am come to destroy the law, or the prophets: I am not come to destroy, but to fulfil. For verily I say unto you, Till Heaven and earth pass, one jot or one tittle shall in no wise pass from the law, till all be fulfilled.' Here is testimony confirmed by an oath, for 'verily' on the lips of the Son of Man carries such force. He affirms the indestructibility of the law, not its substance merely but its form, not the thought but the*

word."

This certainly sounds like Gray believed in the "*preservation*" of the Words of the Bible does it not?

Masoretic Text Not "Imperfect"

STATEMENT #31. (p.33, footnote #11) On the words "*Masoretic Text (MT),*" Sproul wrote this footnote: "*This is the Hebrew text accepted by all believers as the best text, but the 'KJV-only' position claims that it is perfect,*"

COMMENT #31. Why does Sproul drag in his misused and slanderous anti-Ruckmanite term, "*KJV-only,*" when discussing the Hebrew text? This anti-Ruckmanite term cannot logically be used in discussing the Hebrew text, because the Ruckmanites are not concerned about anything but the English King James Bible, which they believe to be a revelation, that supersedes the Hebrew, Aramaic, and Greek Words that underlie it. The Ruckmanites put "*perfection*" at the King James Bible, but I put it at the Hebrew, Aramaic, and Greek Words that underlie it.

"Perfect" Not Used For KJB

STATEMENT #32. (p. 34, footnote #13) Sproul is talking about Blayney's 1769 or Scrivener's 1881: "*If one can never change a single word in that revision, in this case Blayney's 1769 or Scrivener's 1881, because it is 'perfectly preserved,' then the 1611 is not perfect. The 1611 and the 1769 differ, as will be shown later. 'Scrivener's TR' disagrees with other TRs.*"

COMMENT #32. I do not say the "*1611 is . . . perfect.*" I say the Hebrew, Aramaic, and Greek Words underlying the King James Bible are "*perfect.*" Those words are found in "*Scrivener's TR*" which is (with the exception of 190 places) Beza's 5th edition of 1598. I believe these Words to be the preserved, inerrant, infallible, and inspired Words of the originals themselves.

Peter Ruckman's Many Errors

STATEMENT #33. (p. 35) One of Sproul's section headings is as follows with some comments: "*What are the views of the 'KJV-only' perspective? 1. 'The English corrects the Greek is the view of Peter Ruckman;' The title of one of his articles is, 'Why the KJV is Superior to the Originals.'*"

COMMENT #33. Right here Sproul smacks his readers with the heretical "*views*" of Peter Ruckman, and yet includes in the slanderous term, "*KJV-only*" those of us who soundly defend the King James Bible and its underlying Hebrew, Aramaic, and Greek Words. This is what some would call "*dirty pool*" and extreme unfairness. I, and many others like me, despise the heretical view of Ruckman and his followers that the King James Bible "*corrects the Greek*" or Hebrew and that the "*KJV is superior to the Originals.*" The very fact that these trashy views are put by Sproul into the term, *"KJV-only,"* is proof positive why I want nothing to do with such a term. Sproul is an outlaw to the truth by mixing me and others into this poisonous and unscriptural view.

Falsely Tying Us To Ruckman

STATEMENT #34.   (p. 36) Page 36, Sproul writes about some of the men that he wrongly believes should be included in his slanderous *"KJV-only"* position. He lists five positions with names included in #1, 2, 3, and 5. The names included are: *"1. Peter Ruckman . . . 2. Allen Dickerson . . . 3. D. A. Waite . . . David Cloud . . . David Otis Fuller. . . 5. Thomas Strouse."*

COMMENT #34.   By Sproul's placing in his *"KJV-only"* category the name of Peter Ruckman in the first place, together with the names of brothers Dickerson, Waite, Cloud, Fuller, and Strouse, the true purpose of his book is revealed clearly. His purpose is to tar and feather the reputations of the above five men (and others who take a strong anti-Ruckmanite position). He should be ashamed of himself for thus muddying the waters and smearing these good men with the evil brush of Ruckmanism. What he should have done was to have written at least two separate books: (1) one smashing the heresies of Peter Ruckman and (2) another disagreeing with the views of the other anti-Ruckmanite brethren. That would be the honest, ethical, and Christian approach. It is a scandalous shame that Sproul did not take this approach.

Questioning KJB's O.T. Words

STATEMENT #35.   (p. 37, footnote 45) *"The problem for Waite is that two hundred and thirty-two times the KJV does not follow the Masoretic Text in the Old Testament, . . ."*

COMMENT #35.   Sproul is quoting Roy Beacham and Kevin Bauder. Though I have not checked on Sproul's use of the alleged total of *"two hundred and thirty-two times"* that the King James Bible does not follow the *"Masoretic Text,"* let me say the following: There are many Hebrew Bibles that claim to be the *"Masoretic Text."* The *"Masoretic Text"* that I believe to be the preserved Text contains the Hebrew and Aramaic Words underlying the King James Bible. Why should Sproul and his friends want to fight about and be upset about the alleged 232 times where my preferred Hebrew Text differs from their preferred Hebrew Text? Compared to the 610,577 English words in the King James Bible's Old Testament, 232 Words would be only 0.38% of the whole. This percentage is found by dividing 610,577 into 232,000. Do the math!

NKJV--Not Same Hebrew & Greek

STATEMENT #36.   (p. 37, footnote 46) *"The NKJV translation originates from the same Old Testament and New Testament text as the 1611 KJV."*

COMMENT #36. That is a false STATEMENT that has been made by others as well. As I was analyzing the New King James Version (NKJV), quite by accident, I found at least three places in their New Testament where they followed the Critical Greek Text rather than the Textus Receptus. One author I have read claims he found several hundred instances of this. In the NKJV Old Testament, they admit that they followed various sources: (1) The 1967/1977 Stuttgart edition of *Biblia Hebraica*, (2) with comparisons being made with the Bomberg edition of 1524-25; (3) , The Septuagint (Greek) Version of the Old Testament; (4) the Latin Vulgate; (5) referring to a variety of ancient versions of the Hebrew Scriptures; and (6) relevant manuscripts from the Dead Sea caves. (From the Preface of the 1982 study edition of the New King James Version, p. vi). The New King James Version did not have "*the same Old Testament and New Testament text as the 1611 KJV.*"

Translators Did Not "Create" Greek

STATEMENT #37. (p. 37) "*Scrivener's TR Text, however, is the printed Greek text that the KJV translators created in 1611.*" In the same footnote, Sproul wrote: "*Of course, according to Waite, the 1769 KJV was already at the average reading level of any American.*"

COMMENT #37. This is absolutely false. The King James translators did not create Scrivener's text. Dr. Frederick Scrivener stated that the King James Bible is based on Beza's 5th Edition of 1598. In only 190 places did Scrivener indicate where some other edition was followed. Since there are 140,521 Greek Words in the New Testament, 190 places would only amount to 0.14% places that varied from Beza's Greek edition. This would amount to their following of Beza's Greek edition 99.86% of the time. Divide 140,521 into 19,000 and you will get 0.14%. Do the math!

The second part of this above **STATEMENT** is a comment about a research book my son, D. A. Waite, Jr., published in 1996. It is called *The Comparative Readability of the Authorized Version* (BFT #2671 @ $6.00 + $4.00 S&H). This is a readability of seven Bible versions: KJV, ASV, RSV, NASV, NIV, NKJV, & NRSV. It was based on computer research comparing four standard measures of readability current today. On page 38, there is a summary of these seven versions for the entire Bible from the Flesch-Kincaid Grade Level Scores showing all four of the readability current standards. The average for the KJV was a **5.63 grade level**. [The most difficult of the seven (the NASV) had an average of a 6.426 grade level.] Is not the KJV grade level "*at the average reading level of any American*"?

STATEMENT #38. (p. 38) Here Sproul is talking about the fifth group of the so-called only KJV views. "*5. The Last view suggests that, "one finds the correct reading within the multiplicity of TRs. . . . But the proponents of* *this view so strongly deny any association with Ruckman that it does not seem likely that, like Waite and Cloud, they could **hold to the 'exact' perfection of the TR that the KJV translators created**."*

COMMENT #38. Here again Sproul has the incorrect and blatantly false assertion that there is an *"'**exact' perfection of the TR that the KJV translators created**."* Once more Sproul spews out his totally fabricated falsehood that the *"KJV translators created"* a Greek text when, in fact, it was Beza's 5th edition of 1598 that they used. He uses this huge lie to seek to prove that those who, like me, defend the Hebrew, Aramaic, and Greek Words underlying the King James Bible, rather than only the King James Bible, which is based on these Words,--despite our violent opposition to Peter Ruckman's false views--are, in reality, Ruckmanites! Sproul has twisted his logic to justify his slander of good, godly, Fundamentalist brethren!

KJB "Accurate"--Not "Inerrant"

STATEMENT #39. (p. 40) Sproul quotes Dr. Ian Paisley as saying of the King James Bible: *"Being a translation does not alter one iota of its integrity, inerrancy, infallibility as God's Word."* Then he wrote: *"Positionally, this is identical to D. A. Waite or David Cloud's view."*

COMMENT #39. That's from Paisley's *Plea for the Old Sword.* Cloud can speak for himself, but I believe the King James Bible *"does not alter one iota of its integrity . . . as God's Word."* However, though I do not believe the KJB is *"errant"* or *"fallible,"* I reserve the terms, *"inerrant"* and *"infallible"* to the Hebrew, Aramaic, and Greek Words underlying the King James Bible because I believe them to be God's own Words rather than only an English translation of those Words.

NKJV Not Same Greek & Hebrew

STATEMENT #40. (p. 40) *"When a modern translation like the New King James Version **translated from the same Greek and Hebrew text** as the OKJV (Old King James Version) appeared, the attacks came quickly and furiously."*

COMMENT #40. This falsehood has been answered in **COMMENT #36** above.

No "Vilifying" Of People

STATEMENT #41. (p. 40) *". . . in like matter this book understands the KJV-onlyism as more than a simple doctrinal position. It is a spirit or mood. It is a spirit that suspects, vilifies and separates itself from other godly Separatists over the matter of versions."*

COMMENT #41. As I have said often before, *"KJV-onlyism"* is not either an honest or an accurate term because Sproul uses it for five different groups when it should be limited exclusively to Peter Ruckman and his deluded followers. The words might be accurately applied to them. But as for those anti-Ruckmanites like myself whom I have described above, rather than *"separate"* from the Critical Text people, as the Fundamental Baptist Resolution quoted in **COMMENT #20** above makes clear, it is the Bob Jones University followers of the Critical Greek Text that wish to *"reject"* and therefore *"separate"* from those of us whom they termed *"Schismatic 'Brethren.'"* I do not *"suspect, or vilify and separate . . . from other godly Separatists"* as **people**. I do most definitely do so from what I consider to be their **false views and practices** on Bible versions, Bible preservation, and other details of their flawed Bibliology.

I would be very glad to go to Bob Jones University, Detroit Baptist Seminary, Calvary Baptist Seminary, Central Baptist Seminary, Maranatha Baptist Bible College, Northland Baptist Bible College, or any other Critical Text schools like Sproul's to discuss and refute their false views on various Bible issues.

Our Battle Is For the "Words" of God

STATEMENT #42. (p. 41) *"Sadly, an effort to defend their Bible, that they believe is under liberal attack, many pastors and layman have engaged in one of the most divisive and destructive battles among Independent Baptists since the Campbellite controversies of the nineteenth Century and the New Evangelical battles of the twentieth Century."* (A quote from Beacham, p. 49)

COMMENT #42. The battle that we have is for the Words of God. I, the **Bible For Today Baptist Church**, the Bible For Today Ministry, and our Dean Burgon Society all believe that the very original Hebrew, Aramaic, and Greek Words of the Bible have been preserved and kept in their integrity. We have not engaged in a *"divisive and destructive battle."* We have spoken and defended the truth of God's Words. Truth does *"divide"* from untruth and truth does *"destroy"* the false views of those who do not believe and receive it. It is the people like Sproul and others, such as Bob Jones University and the other schools in their network, who have begun this divisiveness by their rejection of the historic position of acceptance of the Hebrew, Aramaic, and Greek Words underlying our King James Bible. They have inserted in their Greek classes teachings that destroy the Words of the Textus Receptus, which underlie our King James Bible. We are not the *"divisive"* ones. We hold the line for our King James Bible that Bible-believing Christians have used down through the centuries and we defend it as the only accurate English translation of the proper Hebrew, Aramaic, and Greek Words which God has preserved for us.

The *"Fundamentals"* Not Infallible

STATEMENT #43. (p. 41) *"It is important for Separatists to understand their history."*

  COMMENT #43. Are the men of *"history"* always right? Are we to worship them as deities? That is one of the subtitles of this book *God's Word Preserved: A Defense of Historic Separatist Definitions and Beliefs.* What if those men were wrong? It is good to have history, but why should we be bound by that *"history"* if that history is wrong? Sproul worships *"history"* to the extent that it cannot be in error on anything. This is man-worship and is a grievous sin. He goes all the way back from 2007 to 1915 when *The Fundamentals* were written. He is exalting the Fundamentalist Fathers with as much authority as the Roman Catholic Church has in the Pope. The Scriptures are clear that we are not to trust in men, but to put our confidence in the Lord and in His Words alone. There are many verses about this, but here are a few:

Proverbs 3:5

Trust in the LORD with all thine heart; and <u>lean not unto thine own understanding.</u>

Matthew 15:9

But in vain they do worship me, <u>teaching *for* doctrines the commandments of men</u>.

Isaiah 8:20

To the law and to the testimony: <u>if they speak not according to this word, *it is* because *there is* no light in them</u>.

1 Corinthians 2:5

That <u>your faith should not stand in the wisdom of men, but in the power of God</u>.

Colossians 2:4

And <u>this I say, lest any man should beguile you with enticing words</u>.

No Ruckmanite "Dual Inspiration"

STATEMENT #44. (p. 41) *"Further he* [that is, Dr. Ian Paisley] *states,* (p. 102) *This new doctrine called Dual Inspiration which affirms that the process extends to the Authorised Version is known as Ruckmanism, after Peter Ruckman who popularized this doctrine, had its beginnings in Rome. . .* <u>*No translation can take the place of the Original autographs of Scripture*</u>.

  COMMENT #44. I agree with Dr. Paisley on this point. I also reject totally the doctrine of *"Dual Inspiration"* and also the so-called *"derivative inspiration"* believed by some of my friends. Peter Ruckman and his many followers are in error in this and many other subjects. We did not have a second inspiration in the 1604-1611 King James Bible. God breathed-out His original Hebrew, Aramaic and Greek Words only and no other languages. I believe these original Hebrew, Aramaic, and Greek Words have been preserved, that they underlie the King James Bible, and that the KJB is the only accurate English translation of them.

CHAPTER TWO: GOD'S INITIAL COMMUNICATION TO MAN (pp. 46-80)

"Fundamentals" Not Our Foundation

STATEMENT #45. (p. 50) *"Sadly, just as Americans are unaware of their founding historical document, that all military officers swear to uphold and defend, so are Fundamentalists unaware of their __founding document__, The Fundamentals, their own history, and its theological discussions. This is the reason this book is written in a historical definitional format."*

      COMMENT #45. If Sproul thinks that *The Fundamentals* are Fundamentalists' "*__founding document__*," he is sadly mistaken. The "*__founding document__*" of Fundamentalists is, or should be, the Bible! This man has no business tying Biblical Christianity to *The Fundamentals* of 1915! Yet he does so through his book. Biblical Christianity must be founded on the Bible. If any part of the 90 Chapters of *The Fundamentals* are outside the Bible, we must resist and repudiate *The Fundamentals*. It is true that the United States Constitution is the basis for the United States Government. It is a man-made document, but it is what the United States of America is to follow. The Bible is the basis for Bible-believing Christians, and that is what they are to follow. Sproul is in deep error when he limits Biblical truth and all truth to a 1915 document. Sproul's worship of this man-made document is serious idolatry! In fact, it is a kind of "Fundamentalist" apostasy! Is this where the so-called "Fundamentalist" world is heading now? I certainly hope not.

1 John 5:21

      Little children, **keep yourselves from idols**. Amen.

Waldenses Had Accurate Translation

STATEMENT #46. (p. 50) *"Did they* [the godly separatists of the Middle Ages] *believe that only one group hidden away in the Alpine Valleys had the only perfect Bible and others might have a good Bible, but only these peasants* *had the __perfect__ Bible?"*

COMMENT #46. Sproul is referring to the Waldenses. I do not use the word *"perfect"* except when speaking of the original and preserved Hebrew, Aramaic, and Greek Words underlying our King James Bible. This is a term I reserve for our Triune God, what He does, and the Words that He breathed-out. I do believe that the Waldenses had a Bible that was founded on the Traditional Received Text.

Inerrant "Words" Are Preserved

STATEMENT #47. (p. 51) *"In its broadest sense, special revelation includes the entire __content__ of all 66 books of the Bible that God moved upon the holy men of old to write. Since this revelation as a work of God Himself, it should be presumed that God's __Word__ is absolute truth with no mixture of any error. . . . Specific revelation speaks to __the very Words__ of Scripture."*

COMMENT #47. I do not know what Sproul believes about the preservation of the Words of the Bible. When he uses *"content"* and *"Word"* at first, it sounds to me that he believes similarly to Bob Jones University and agrees with the other books they have written on this subject where, when talking about Bible preservation, the *"__Word__ of God"* means only the *"ideas, thoughts, concepts, message, truth, or teachings"* of God but not the preservation of God's literal *"Words."* Though he states that *"specific __revelation__ speaks to __the very Words__ of Scripture,"* he does not clarify what he thinks *"specific preservation"* includes. And this is an important thing to find out. Sproul's specific beliefs on this will come out later in his book.

Not Only the "Originals" Are Perfect

STATEMENT #48. (p. 53) *"Fundamentalists accept the doctrine of perfection of the original writings. However, sometimes those in the 'KJV-only' movement diminish this perfection. A 'KJV-only' pastor once said, 'It does not really matter whether the original writings were perfect or not. No one today has ever seen them.'"*

COMMENT #48. It certainly *"matters whether the original writings were perfect or not*, but if those original Hebrew, Aramaic, and Greek Words were not preserved (as I believe that they were), that would leave us without a sure foundation for the details of our doctrines. This would be a serious situation.

"Great Men" Can Often Be Wrong

STATEMENT #49. (p. 53) *"Sadly, this pastor does know enough about his own history to understand that he is attacking his Fundamentalist Fathers by mimicking and adopting the liberal's line of argument against those great men."*

COMMENT #49. Again, Sproul is putting his *"Fundamentalist Fathers"* on the pedestal of impeccability rather than the Bible. Who are these *"Fundamentalist Fathers"* that we cannot argue against them if and when they are in error? Are they perfect? He may as well worship the Pope and the canonized Roman Catholic *"saints."* If he has a human standard instead of the Words of God as his standard, he is in deep trouble. This is idolatry by worshiping men rather than worshiping God.

Denial of "Words" Preservation

STATEMENT #50. (p. 55) *"Many in the 'KJV-only' Movement assert preservation and inspiration in near identical language and in so doing are willing to lump preservation into a 'faith' issue, but preservation is different than creation or the Virgin Birth for it is repeatable and observable."*

COMMENT #50. What is wrong with having *"preservation and inspiration in near identical language"*? Why not? God gave us His Words in the Bible by verbal plenary inspiration. He preserved His Words in the Bible by verbal plenary preservation. There is no problem with asserting these things on an equal footing. If the Almighty God of the Bible was not able to verbally and plenarily preserve His original Words of the Bible, how can we be sure that he was able to verbally and plenarily inspire His original Words of the Bible? The simple answer is that He has done both of these actions. As I wrote in **Comment #30** above, the Lord Jesus Christ said: *"Heaven and earth shall pass away, but my Words shall __not__ pass away"* (Matthew 24:35; Mark 13:31; and Luke 21:33). The Greek term for *"not"* is OU ME. This is the strongest Greek negative particle in the language. It means *"never, never."* This is an unmistakable promise of the *"preservation"* of the Bible's Hebrew, Aramaic, and Greek Words.

STATEMENT #51. (p. 56) *"The location of God's __preserved Word__ is never specifically stated in Scripture other than it is in heaven (Psalm 119:89)."*

COMMENT #51. Notice that Sproul talks about *"God's preserved __Word__"* rather than *"God's preserved __Words__."* Like his Critical Text sister schools and pastors, he refers only to the *"ideas, thoughts, concepts, message, truth, or teachings"* of God rather than to His exact Words. As stated in **STATEMENTS** #20 and #50 above, the Words are preserved in the proper manuscripts that have been copied from the originals (Matthew 24:35; Mark 13:31; and Luke 21:33). Psalm 119:89 states that God's Words are *"settled in Heaven."* In Hebrew, the phrase, *"in Heaven,"* is BaSHAMAIM. The "Ba" represents the Hebrew letter BETH which can be understood as either *"in"* or *"by."* The Words have been settled *"by"* Heaven and they were settled *"in"* Heaven even before they were written down on earth.

Sproul's **STATEMENT** doubting the *"location of God's preserved Word"* makes him an agnostic concerning Bible preservation. The *"location"* is found in the Received Words underlying the King James Bible rather than in his favored but depraved Critical Text Words changed in 1881 by heretics Westcott and Hort. I certainly would not want to sit under a pastor who did not know the *"location of God's preserved Word."*

"Double Inspiration" False Charge

STATEMENT #52. (pp. 56-57 and footnote #74) Sproul had this heading: *"Does inspiration extend to copies either in Greek or in English?"* He followed by these words: *"Some critics of Fundamentalism's historic interpretation of Scripture concerning inspiration and its extent, like D. A. Waite, claim the KJV translators adopted 'exact' word choice, double inspiration of the original authors of Scripture as they created a 'new' edition of the Textus Receptus that would be the basis of the 1611 KJV."* Footnote #74 appeared after the word, *"double inspiration."* The footnote read: *"**Double inspiration is a position that believes God extended inspiration a second time to the KJV translators' choices in English in the same manner as He originally inspired the word choices of John or Paul.** Waite rejects the mantle of Ruckmanism."*

COMMENT #52. First, this is a blatant and libelous falsehood (and I believe Sproul knows it to be) to claim that I believe in *"double inspiration."* That is a Ruckmanite belief that I have rejected repeatedly in tapes, videos, and in print.

Second, the *"KJV translators"* did not *"create a 'new' edition of the Textus Receptus."*

I have explained in **COMMENTS #37 and #66** the Greek text on which the King James Bible translators relied. It was Beza's 5th edition, 1598. This is NOT a text of their own creation and Sproul knows it. Sproul recognized that I *"reject the mantle of Ruckmanism,"* and yet he slanders me with the Ruckmanite heresy of *"double inspiration."*

TR Under KJB Is the Purest

STATEMENT #53. (p. 56) *"In his article on D. A. Waite's website, Jeffrey Khoo writes, 'We believe that all the TR editions are pure, but there is one that is purest--the one underlying the KJV.'"*

CONTENT #53. Dr. Khoo is the Academic Dean of the Far Eastern Bible College and Theological Seminary and a Bible Presbyterian Pastor in Singapore. I have known him since 1992. I agree with Dr. Khoo's opinion. Does he not have a right to believe, as I do, that the *"one that is purest"* is *"the one underlying the KJV"*?

Words Under KJB Not New TR Text

STATEMENT #54. (p. 56) *"This is a 'KJV-only' author admitting that the KJV translators made text critical choices to <u>create a completely new text</u> not in front of them, and was original to them."*

CONTENT #54. That is absolutely false. I explain in **COMMENT #37 and #66** about the Greek text on which the King James Bible translators relied. It was not *"a completely new text,"* but was basically Beza's 5th edition of 1598. The King James translators used an existing Greek text. They did not create it or invent their Greek text. Sproul wants so badly to slander all of his opponents, and put them all into the Ruckmanite box, that he viciously lies about the Words underlying the King James Bible so as to lead his gullible readers astray.

KJB Translators Not "Inspired"

STATEMENT #55. (p. 57) *"If the KJV translators choices <u>created a 'new edition' of the TR</u> that is the 'right' one, is this not 'double inspiration'? Is this not Ruckmanism? <u>Khoo believes that God inspired the translators to create a 'new edition'</u> of the TR by their Word choices in the English."*

COMMENT #55. This is absolutely false!

The KJV translators did not *"create a 'new edition' of the TR,"* they merely translated basically from Beza's 5th edition text of 1598. There is not one ounce of *"double inspiration"* in the KJB translation. That is Ruckmanite talk! The translators did not believe in this, nor do I, nor does Dr. Khoo. Only the Ruckmanites believe in it and this is why Sproul seeks to slander people and lie about this matter in order to make Dr. Khoo and me, and all the rest of those who oppose him, into Ruckmanites in order to smear and tar our good names and reputations. It is one of the dirtiest tricks imaginable by a presumably honest Baptist minister of the Gospel!

Dr. Khoo does not believe the King James Bible translators *"created a 'new edition."* And he certainly does not hold the heresy that Sproul holds that *"God inspired the translators."* The phrase, *"given by inspiration of God"* is a translation of the Greek word, THEOPNEUSTOS. It means literally *"God-breathed"* as I have mentioned several times above. God breathed out WORDS, not writers, authors, or translators like Sproul's heresy on *"inspiration"* believes. Sproul is a Baptist Fundamentalist Christian believer, and yet he is publishing distortions, falsehoods, and outright lies. This is a disgrace!

STATEMENT #56. (p. 58) *"If the KJV, or the TR behind the 1611, has the 'exact' words of God, yet <u>the translators' 'exact' text never appeared before 1611</u>, then <u>inspiration is the only method</u> by which the Holy Spirit could have guided the Anglican Priests to the 'exact' wording of Scripture when they had* *many choices in various passages."*

COMMENT #56. There are many false statements here. (1) As I have said before, the translators of the King James Bible had a Greek text in their hands that was Beza's 5th edition compiled in 1598, thirteen years before 1611. (2) It is ridiculous and stupid for Sproul to say that "*inspiration is the only method*" that could lead them to their translation! They used Beza's Textus Receptus Greek edition and through their wisdom and understanding (**not** the "*inspiration*" of God the Holy Spirit as was used in the original Old and New Testaments) they chose (as mentioned in **STATEMENT #37** above) 190 places out of 140,521 Greek Words in the New Testament (0.14%) to follow some other sources and 99.86% following Beza's 5th edition, 1598.

Preserved "Words" Under the KJB

STATEMENT #57. (p. 58) *"Waite wrote, 'It is my own personal conviction and belief, after studying this subject since 1971, that the Words of the Received Greek and Masoretic Hebrew Texts that underlie the King James Bible are the **very** [author's emphasis] Words which God has preserved down through the centuries, being the **exact** [author's emphasis] Words of the originals themselves. As such, I believe they are inspired words. I believe they are preserved words. I believe they are inerrant words. I believe they are infallible Words.'"*

In Sproul's footnote #28 (p. 58) he wrote: *"This statement of Waite refers to the TR behind the 1611 KJV. Ruckman asserts that the KJV translators were perfect in their English choices."*

COMMENT #57. I am glad, for a change, that Sproul quoted me exactly, and at length. I certainly agree with my own statement. From this statement, since I believe the original Words of the Bible have been Preserved for us, Sproul knows what I mean when I call these Words "*inspired*," "*Preserved*," "*inerrant*," and "*infallible*." I am referring to the Hebrew, Aramaic, and Greek Words underlying the King James Bible. I do not use these terms in referring to the King James Bible itself. Knowing this, Sproul continues to slander me, libel me, and lie about me by saying that I am a follower of Peter Ruckman and that I believe in the Ruckmanite heresy of "*double inspiration.*" Nothing could be further from the truth!

In Sproul's footnote #28 (p. 58) he mentions that my statement was from my book, *Defending the King James Bible*, pp. 48-49. His words wrongly attempted to imply that my views were identical to those of Peter Ruckman, thus slanderously and libelously making me a Ruckmanite. He implies that my view of the Greek text underlying the King James Bible is identical with his. Ruckman doesn't need any Greek text because he believes the heresy that the King James Bible is a direct revelation from God the Holy Spirit, including the italics, and therefore the words of that Bible were given verbally and plenarily by God the

Holy Spirit. Thus the translators had really nothing to do with it. Ruckman teaches that God put the English words, including the italics, into their minds and then on their pens. This is ridiculous heretical foolishness without an iota of Biblical basis! For Sproul to attempt, by slick implication, to equate me with this Biblical heresy is indeed both disgusting and reprehensible! Shame on him!

No "Inspiration" For KJB "Choices"

STATEMENT #58. (p. 58) *"D. A. Waite asserts that the <u>inspiration extends to the KJV translators' choices</u> of the '<u>new edition' of the TR</u> that they made when they translated the KJV as well as the Masoretic Text."*

COMMENT #58. Sproul just quoted my belief in **STATEMENT #57** above, and then he falsely states that I *"assert that the inspiration extends to the KJV translators' choices of the 'new edition' of the TR."* Please let him tell me where I *"assert"* that. I repeat once again, the *"KJV translators"* did not make a *"'new edition' of the TR,"* and Sproul knows it. He insists on putting forth his heretical view of the *"inspiration"* of people rather than, as it must be, of the Hebrew, Aramaic, and Greek Words. He makes this lying, slanderous, and libelous charge against me to attempt to prove to his readers that I am a Ruckmanite and that I believe in *"double inspiration,"* both of which charges are false.

KJB Translators Not "Perfect"

STATEMENT #59. (p. 58) *"Based on his attacks on the NKJV and articles on his websites, <u>Waite apparently extends this 'exact' perfection to the KJV translators</u> because <u>they created their own TR</u> when they translated."*

COMMENT #59. This is one more absolute falsehood. I do not extend *"perfection to the KJV translators.* They were just imperfect fallen creatures like the rest of mankind. The *"TR"* or Textus Receptus is a document in the Greek language. If Sproul has uncovered any such Greek document *"created"* by the King James Bible translators, let him produce it! He cannot do it, because it does not exist now, nor has it ever existed. One more example of Sproul's twisted logic, reason, and fact.

STATEMENT #60. (pp. 58-59) *"D. A. Waite says <u>the translators were 'exact'</u> in their choices of the Greek words to underlie their English text so that these choices are the '<u>exact words of the originals themselves</u>.'"*

COMMENT #60. Sproul is twisting my words once again. I did not say <u>the translators were 'exact.'</u> I did not say they were *"**inspired**"* as Sproul falsely charges Dr. Khoo in **STATEMENT #55** above. Sproul is removing my clear use of *"exact"* from *"exact words of the originals themselves"* to *"exact"* translators. He does not agree with me on this. He does not know where the *"words of the originals"* are located, but he should not misquote me on my firm "*personal conviction and belief.*" He doesn't know where they are. Sproul claims he follows the "Majority Text" position (which challenges the Textus Receptus Words in over 1,800 places), but he favors the Critical Text (which challenges the Textus Receptus Words in over 8,000 places) in many of his comments.

False Charge of "Double Inspiration"

STATEMENT #61. (p. 59)   "*This is the teaching of <u>double inspiration</u>.*"

COMMENT #61. This totally false statement is a conclusion based on my **COMMENT #60** which he completely twisted. Because Sproul believes in the heresy of the "*inspiration*" of **people** rather than **Words**, and he says that I believe in the "*inspiration*" of the King James Bible translators (which I do not), he makes the slanderous and libelous conclusion that I believe in "*double inspiration*" (which I do not). Apparently Sproul will stop at nothing in his hateful attitude toward me and others like me who are adamantly opposed to the teachings of Peter Ruckman and his terminology. I deny and oppose any belief in the "*inspiration*" of the KJB translators. I deny and oppose belief in "*double inspiration.*" We believe in the verbal plenary preservation of the original Hebrew, Aramaic, and Greek Words which is neither Ruckmanism nor "*double inspiration.*" Sproul knows this, but insists on twisting truth and creating lies, falsehoods, slanders, and libels against any who disagree with his erroneous positions. In my studied opinion, this kind of distortion disqualifies Sproul from being either a Fundamentalist Baptist pastor or the Chairman of the Board of his Fundamentalist International Baptist College.

STATEMENT #62. (p. 59)   "*Play with word definitions all that one may, call it 'providential oversight' or 'providential preservation,' but when those terms refer to an exactly perfect 1611 (KJV) or 1769 revision or a 1517, or 1598, or 1633, or 1881 TR, then one is really and <u>truly teaching double inspiration</u> of the translators' product . . .*"

COMMENT #62. Sproul is purposely confusing verbal plenary preservation of the original Hebrew, Aramaic, and Greek Words with the "Inspiration" of those Words. He is also purposely confusing the true meaning of Biblical "*inspiration.*" It does not refer to any translation, including the King James Bible. It does not refer to "*inspired men,*" whether it is the original prophets and apostles, or to the King James translators. It refers solely to the original Hebrew, Aramaic, and Greek Words and to those verbal plenary preserved Words which we have today. There is no such thing as "*double inspiration*" which Sproul talks about. God breathed out or "*inspired*" the Hebrew, Aramaic, and Greek Words of our Bible only once. None of the editions mentioned by Sproul in 1611, 1769, 1517, 1598,

1633, or 1881 were "*given by inspiration of God*" or God-breathed! It is foolish to consider that they were. This false view of "*inspiration*" held by Sproul is one of his major heresies and misconceptions on which he builds his various slanders and libels of me and others.

God's Words Available From the First

STATEMENT #63. (pp. 59-60) *"Were all the godly Christians from the time of John and Paul bereft of the 'exact' Greek NT of the Holy Spirit until Scrivener placed the KJV translators' words back in a Greek text in 1881. How could God allow the 'exact' Greek words of the originals to be inaccessible to eighteen centuries of Christians?"*

COMMENT #63. No one is saying that these "*godly Christians*" were "*bereft*" of "*Greek NT.*" Of course, John and Paul were "*bereft*" of it because it was not completed during their lifetimes. Sproul is in serious error when he alleges that "*Scrivener placed the KJV translators' words back in a Greek text in 1881.*" He completely misrepresents what Dr. Frederick Scrivener did. **COMMENT #37 and #66** explain correctly what Dr. Scrivener did. Sproul has lied about this matter as he has done repeatedly through his book.

No Translation English to Greek

STATEMENT #64. (p. 60) Sproul wrote, *". . . only after 1881, when Scrivener put those English choices into Greek, were pastors and scholars able to have the 'purest' Greek text that identically matches the original?"*

COMMENT #64. Once again, Sproul has lied about what Dr. Scrivener did. He did not *put those English choices into Greek*. He did what I mention under **COMMENT #37 and #66.** Rather, he ascertained what Greek Words the King James translators translated and not the other way around. As for my belief in the *'purest' Greek text that identically matches the original*, Sproul quoted it in his **STATEMENT #57** above. I did not quote Scrivener anywhere in the statement, nor did I imply that this is anyone else's belief but my own. Sproul took it from my book, *Defending the King James Bible*, pp. 48-49. Let me repeat it:

> *"It is my own personal conviction and belief, after studying this subject since 1971, that the Words of the Received Greek and Masoretic Hebrew Texts that underlie the King James Bible are the very* [author's emphasis]*Words which God has preserved down through the centuries, being the exact* [author's emphasis] *Words of the originals themselves. As such, I believe they are inspired words. I believe they are preserved words. I believe they are inerrant words. I believe they are infallible Words."*

I do not know how I can be any clearer that this "*my own personal conviction and belief.*" He can either be uncertain of the Words God has preserved (which I believe that he is); or he can rest on the false Westcott and Hort/Critical Text manuscripts; or he can rest on his false "Majority Text" that he claims to believe. I speak only for myself in the above quotation.

STATEMENT #65.   (p. 60)   Sproul again mentions his blatant lie when he wrote, ". . . *in 1881, when Scrivener converted the KJV translators' choices into Greek.*"

COMMENT #65. How can Sproul say this lying falsehood? Dr. Scrivener never did anything of the sort. Where is his proof of this? This is pure speculation without a shred of evidence or proof. What Scrivener really did I explain in my **COMMENT #37 and #66**.

STATEMENT #66.   (p. 61)   "*. . . the exact original text was not accessible in one place until 1881 when Scrivener placed the KJV translators' choices in Greek.*"

COMMENT #66. Again this is a boldfaced lie. How can this saved man use the tactics of the Devil? I am not calling him a devil. I am wondering why this saved, Bible believing, Fundamentalist man, who is going to Heaven the same as I am, use the methods of the Devil and repeatedly employ lies in his book.

Dr. Scrivener did NOT translate the English into Greek. The University of Cambridge asked Dr. Scrivener to do two things. (1) First, they wanted him to get out a Greek edition that underlies the King James Bible. He did that. He used Beza's Text, the 5th edition of 1598, and put that in print for the University of Cambridge as they requested. (2) Secondly, they wanted him to show by clear means the changes that the 1881 English Revised Version had done to the Greek. They wanted the Westcott and Hort false Greek Text to be shown clearly. That is what Dr. Scrivener did in bold letters. He also showed in the footnotes how the Textus Receptus had been changed by the critical text.

New Greek Text Not "Created"

STATEMENT #67. (p. 62) "*Instead of having a Greek text and then translating it into English, they first created a new Greek text, from their English version and, in so doing, created the 'exact' Greek text that Khoo deems 'perfect' but from their English translation choices.*"

COMMENT #67. Again Sproul shows he is the master of "*bearing false witness*" (Exodus 20:16; Deuteronomy 5:20; Matthew 19:18; Romans 13:9) and lying. He has no factual evidence whatsoever for his slanderous and libelous statement that: "*Instead of having a Greek text and then* _translating it into English, they first created a new Greek text_" This is another example of this Fundamentalist, Bible believing man, who is the pastor of Tri-State Baptist Church in Tempe, Arizona making use of the Devil's tactics of lying (John 8:44). The Devil is the father of lies and Sproul is lying on his and many other occasions.

STATEMENT #68. (p. 62) _"Many 'KJV-only' advocates claim perfection, not for the English translation, but rather for the TR that 'underlies' the KJV because they do not want to appear that they agree with Ruckman. However, both the English translation and the Greek text production happened at the same time by the same men."_

COMMENT #68. This is another one of Sproul's blatant lies. He again falsely states that the "_Greek text production_" was made by the King James Bible translators, when in fact, they never made such a "_Greek text._" As explained fully in my **COMMENT #37 and #66**, the King James Bible translators used basically Beza's 5th edition, 1598, rather than producing a Greek text. Sproul would have an impossible time of coming up with such a phantom Greek text because it never existed, and he should know this. Again Sproul seeks to brand me and others like me with the slanderous labels of "KJV-only" and Ruckmanism, both which I reject adamantly as I have mentioned repeatedly.

KJB & NKJV Greek Text Not Same

STATEMENT #69. (pp. 62-63) _". . . the NKJV uses the same TR choices as the original KJV to underlie its English renderings."_

COMMENT #69. Though it is claimed by the editors of the New King James Version that they use the same Greek text as the King James Bible, I have found at least three places where they do not. Someone recently told me that he found other places as well.

No TR "Creation"

STATEMENT #70. (p. 63) _"It appears that the arguments by the 'KJV-only' position for a perfect '__KJV translation created TR__' are really a discussion to divert attention so they can preserve Blayney's 1769 revision of the KJV while avoiding any association with Ruckman."_

COMMENT #70. I do not try to "_divert attention_" about anything. When Sproul uses the phrase, '_KJV translation created TR,_' he is once again distorting the facts. The translators did not "_create_" the Greek text that underlies the King James Bible. This is an outright lie. They followed Beza's 5th edition of 1598.

"Double Inspiration"--A False Charge

STATEMENT #71. (p. 63) _"The teaching of some 'KJV-only' leaders_ that 'Scrivener's TR is exactly the same as the autograph' appears to allow the novice to hold the 'KJV-only' position without identification with Ruckman and double inspiration."

COMMENT #71. Again, I refuse to adopt the slanderous term of "*KJV-only*" because of its association with Peter Ruckman's heretical views including "*double inspiration.*"

STATEMENT #72. (p. 63) "*Yet, the same translators, whom Ruckman claims are perfect in the English choices, receive reverence in **Waite** and Cloud's **wing of the 'KJV-only' movement** as perfect as those Greek and Hebrew choices. What is the difference? In actuality **both views give double inspiration powers to the Anglican priest's product**.*"

COMMENT #72. I am not a "*wing of the 'KJV-only' movement*"! I decry it and have nothing to do with it. As for the impossible charge or my believing in "*double inspiration*," see my **COMMENT #55** above. Sproul is misusing once again the process of "*inspiration*," attributing it to men rather than to the original Words of the Bible. "Anglican priests" could not "*inspire*" anything, only God Himself could do that! More of his heresy!

No "Error" Was Claimed

STATEMENT #73. (p. 63, footnote #44) quoting from Charles MacClain in the *Calvary Baptist Theological Journal*, (Spring/Fall 1996), Sproul wrote: "*This is an excellent article refuting Thomas M. Strouse, who would encourage Christians to **believe that the KJV is in error** and that 'in' should really be translated 'by' in Psalm 119:89.*"

COMMENT #73. He is referring to "*in Heaven*" versus "*by Heaven*." Both are possible with the Hebrew letter "*Beth.*" Dr. Strouse does not claim this is an error any more than I do when I make the same point. God's Words are "*settled in and by Heaven*" both. The falsehood here is that Dr. Strouse by no means "***believes that the KJV is in error***" by merely suggesting another rendering which is possible. There is nothing wrong with that choice.

No "Inspiration" For 1611 Work

STATEMENT #74. (p. 64) "*If the translators' choices are the 'exact' words of the original, then **God equally inspired the 1611 translators' work** as he did James' or Moses'.*"

COMMENT #74. This is absolutely false. The Lord did not "***inspire the translators' work***." This is a stupid and ridiculous statement that does not befit Sproul. It is because of his heretical view of "inspiration" that he makes these inane statements. God did not "*breathe out*" or "*inspire*" His Words as a process more than one time. That occurred when the original Hebrew, Aramaic, and Greek Words were given by God to the human writers. He is totally in error also when he implies that "*James*" or "*Moses*" were "*inspired*." The only things that were "*inspired or God-breathed*" were the Words that God gave James and Moses to write down in the Bible. I would suggest that Sproul take another beginning course in Biblical Theology and study when the inspiration of the Bible took place, how it took place, and what was involved. Sproul is a perfect illustration of what God promised would happen "*in the last days*":

"*But evil men and seducers shall wax worse and worse, deceiving, and being deceived.*" (2 Timothy 3:13)

Indeed, Michael Sproul is both "*deceiving, and being deceived*" in his heresy of "*inspiration.*" He should repent of this false teaching!

"Double Inspiration"--False Charge

STATEMENT #75. (p. 65) "*If the answer to the 'why' is because the 1611 translators did it, then that is the double inspiration of Ruckman, not in English, but in Greek.*"

COMMENT #75. Again, this is Sproul's foolish and heretical view of the "*inspiration*" of **people**, in this case, the "*1611 translators.*" I guess I will have to refute this heresy every time he states it throughout his book. He desperately needs this heretical lie in order to falsely make me and other strongly anti-Ruckmanites to be Ruckmanites, even though we are not, by any true analysis of the question. Again by his false and heretical view of "*inspiration*," Sproul is saying we believe in his kind of "*double inspiration*," when we do not. God did not breathe out English words. He only breathed out Hebrew, Aramaic, and Greek words.

"Translators" Not "Perfect"

STATEMENT #76. (pp. 65-66) "*Because the translators are declared perfect, according to Waite and Khoo, no one can ever touch the TR of the King James translators' creation because believers have used it for many years and the blessing of God is evident on this translation.*"

COMMENT #76. I do not "*declare the translators perfect*" and Sproul cannot find anywhere either in print or on tape where I have done so. Nor do I think he can find any evidence that Dr. Khoo believes this either. But then, liars need no documentation, do they? Just bold and repetitive assertion will do just fine for their evil and wicked goals. The translators had a fallen sinful nature like the rest of humanity. As for "*the TR of the King James translators' creation,*" I have said many times earlier, these translators did not "*create*" a TR, but used basically Beza's 5th edition, 1598. Sproul is way off on both his facts and his reasoning.

"Word" of God Not "Words" of God

STATEMENT #77. (p. 66) Quoting Dr. Jeffrey Khoo the Dean of the Far Eastern Bible College and Seminary, Sproul wrote: *"'Bob Jones University and Calvary Baptist Theological Seminary, as well as White, Kutilek, Price, and Hudson do not believe in inerrancy and believe that the Bible only 'contains' the Word of God.' This claim is not true. His claim is a sad example of either willful ignorance or dishonesty."*

COMMENT #77. On the contrary, all of the schools and individuals mentioned above deny that we have the original Hebrew, Aramaic, and Greek Words preserved to this day inerrantly. They claim there are errors in those Words today and that therefore, we do not have an *"inerrant"* Hebrew, Aramaic, and Greek Bible. Their Bible only *"contains"* some of the Words of God here and there, but they cannot tell which are the Words and which are not the Words of God. They believe that only the *"ideas, thoughts, concepts, message, truth, or teachings"* of the original Words are preserved rather than the *"Words"* themselves. Their *"Bible"* is one with *"scribal errors"* scattered throughout the Old and New Testaments.

The KJB–No Relation to the Pope

STATEMENT #78. (p. 67) *"This Pope's belief in a perfect version, which is so similar to KJV Onlyism, is refuted in the preface to the KJV."*

COMMENT #78. He is talking about Pope Sixtus V and the Latin Vulgate. He says this is similar to the way people believe about the KJV. Though Ruckmanites believe in the *"perfection"* of the KJB translation, I do not use this term for it. I believe it is an *"accurate"* translation of the preserved original Hebrew, Aramaic, and Greek Words.

Though I do not believe there are any translational errors, I use the word *"perfect"* for the originals and their preserved copies. Only God is *"perfect."* *"As for God His way is perfect"* (Psalm 18:30).

New King James Version Dangers

STATEMENT #79. (p. 67) This is one of Sproul's footnotes about me: "In *Defending the King James Bible*, p. 125, Waite says, 'The diabolical [author's emphasis] *nature of the New King Version shows itself in their printing all of the various readings of the Greek text in the footnotes.'"*

COMMENT #79. It is *"diabolical"* because, in its study edition, it prints in the footnotes *"all of the various readings of the Greek text."* Satan is a master of confusion, and the printing of *"all"* readings is confusing as to which ones they believe to be the true and which to be the false. The average

Christian does not know which of the readings to believe. I believe the Greek Words underlying the King James Bible are the only true ones. All other readings are in error. Printing truth and error without discernment is indeed "*diabolical.*"

KJB Translators Not "Inspired"

STATEMENT #80. (p. 68) Sproul puts a question in the center of the page that says: *"Did the KJV translators believe in their own inspiration?"*

   COMMENT #80.   Sproul is in total error on his use of "*inspiration*" here as elsewhere. Please refer back to my **COMMENT #55** for a complete explanation of "*inspiration*" and Sproul's heresy on it. It refers only to the Words given by God, but never to people.

No "New Edition TR" for KJB

STATEMENT #81.   Referring to the KJB translators, Sproul asked: *"Did they believe their __new edition TR__ or their __English translation__ was __inspired or perfect?__"*

   COMMENT #81. Sproul repeats his error on his phantom "__new edition TR__" which the KJB translators never produced. Again Sproul repeats his heresy and misunderstanding of "*inspiration*." God did not breathe out English, Spanish, French, or any other language but Hebrew, Aramaic, and Greek. These are the only "*God-breathed*" or "*inspired*" Words in existence. Look at **COMMENT #55** above for more on this.

Translators Not "Divinely Inspired"

STATEMENT #82. (p. 71)   *"Did the KJV translators believe __their work was as divinely inspired as were the apostles and prophets__ in either their Greek, Hebrew or English word choices."*

> **COMMENT #82.** The King James translators did not believe "__their work was . . . divinely inspired,__" nor do I. Only Ruckmanites hold to this heretical view. Nor "__were the apostles and prophets__" in any way "__divinely inspired.__" This is the heresy that Sproul has repeated elsewhere. Divine inspiration concerns how God breathed-out or "*inspired*" His __WORDS__. God did not breathe out "*apostles and prophets*" or any other __PEOPLE__.

No "Inerrant" Translations/Versions

STATEMENT #83. (p. 74) This is under the heading, *"What Did Early Fundamentalists Believe About Inerrancy."* *"The early Fundamentalist fathers never extended this belief of an inerrant and infallible autograph to translations* *and versions."*

> **COMMENT #83.** Neither do I use the words "*inerrant*" or "*infallible*" for "*translations and versions*." I believe that these words should only be used for the autographs and the Hebrew, Aramaic, and Greek copies (apographs) underlying the King James Bible which I believe to be plenarily and verbally preserved.

STATEMENT #84. (p. 75). This is a quotation from James Gray: "*There is no translation absolutely without error.*"

> **COMMENT #84.** Though I refuse to use the words "*inerrant*" or "*infallible*" for the King James Bible, I have said many times before, and I believe, that there are no "*translational errors*" in the King James Bible. I believe the translators used at least one of the correct English words and at least one of the correct grammatical rules in their translation, though other correct words and other correct grammatical rules could have also been used.

STATEMENT #85. (p. 78) Sproul has a heading that reads: "*Should the views of the <u>Fathers of Fundamentalism</u> shape the nature of the discussion?*"

> **COMMENT #85.** I do not think that we should let the "<u>*Fathers of Fundamentalism*</u>" guide our discussion of Biblical truth. The Bible itself should do this. They were not infallible in their judgments about the Bible in 1915. Though we would agree with many of their writings, these men should not take the place of the Words of God for our authority.

TR Not Based on Only Seven MSS

STATEMENT #86. (p. 79 footnote 100) Referring to the so-called "*Majority text*," Sproul wrote: "*This text-type depends upon over four thousand manuscripts, while its much small daughter, the TR, relies on only <u>seven manuscripts.</u>*"

> **COMMENT #86.** This is completely false again. Sproul refers to Erasmus as having only "*seven manuscripts*" as if these samples comprised the entire Received Text. Of the total of 5,255 Greek manuscripts available to Kurt Aland in Munster, Germany in 1967, according to Dr. Jack Moorman in his book, *Forever Settled*, the manuscripts going along with the Textus Receptus number 5,210 or <u>99.14%</u> of the preserved evidence, whereas the 45 critical text manuscripts would amount to only <u>0.86%</u> of the preserved evidence. In point of fact, the so-called "*Majority text*" of Hodges and Farstad relied on Von Soden's meager 414 manuscripts rather than "*four thousand.*"

The "KJV TR" Not "Completely New"

STATEMENT #87. (p. 80) Speaking of the "*KJV translators*," Sproul wrote: "*They created a new Textus Receptus which while it was in the stream of other very similar Greek printed texts, it was not identical to any of them before it, and only became known as the Textus Receptus twenty-two years after the translators finished their work in 1611. Scrivener placed these English choices in Greek two hundred seventy years later. The KJV TR was a completely new edition.*"

COMMENT #87. Sproul keeps repeating this totally false statement saying that the KJV translators "created a new Textus Receptus." They did nothing of the kind. They merely translated Beza's 5th edition of 1598 in all but 190 places (only 0.14% of the time). Since there are 140,521 words in the Greek New Testament (if my math is correct), they used Beza's already in existence Greek edition 99.86% of the time. They most definitely did NOT "create a new Textus Receptus.." This is a blatant lie on Sproul's part without one syllable of documentation to prove it.

CHAPTER THREE: GOD'S COMMUNICATION THROUGH THE GENERATIONS (pp. 81-139)

"Absolute Perfection" Promised

STATEMENT #88. (p. 83) This begins Chapter Three which is entitled: *"God's Communication Through the Generations: Definitions Concerning Transmission of Text."* Sproul wrote: *"Conservative Separatists have historically believed that the original documents of Scripture were perfect, but that <u>absolute perfection did not extend to copies of the original language documents</u> or translations into the scores of languages around the world."*

COMMENT #88. Are *"Conservative Separatists"* always correct? Not necessarily. I prefer to believe the Lord Jesus Christ's Words which are repeated exactly in Matthew, Mark and Luke, *"Heaven and earth shall pass away, but my words shall not pass away"* (Matthew 24:35; Mark 13:31; Luke 21:33). The word for *"not"* is OU ME which is the strongest negative in the Greek language. The Lord Jesus Christ is the Author of all the New Testament Greek Words (John 16:12-14). As the Revelator and Logos, I believe He is also the Author of all the Old Testament Hebrew and Aramaic Words. To say that His words will *"not pass away"* means that there will be a preservation of those Words right down to the present and on into the future. While others might believe these Words have been preserved elsewhere, I believe, for a number of good reasons and facts, that the Words are those Hebrew, Aramaic, and Greek Words that underlie our King James Bible.

No "Double Inspiration"

STATEMENT #89. (p. 83 and footnote 2) This is under the section entitled *"Transcription."* Sproul wrote: *"Transcription is the process of a faithful* *scribe making trusted copies of Greek, Hebrew and Aramaic.*" In his footnote #2, he wrote: "*With these presuppositions, the 'KJV-only' advocates must accept either <u>one document copied perfectly for 1500 years</u> or the <u>double inspiration of the KJV translators' translation</u> to restore perfection to the world.*"

COMMENT #89. I do not believe in "<u>double inspiration of the KJV translators' translation.</u>" This is ridiculous and is pure Ruckmanistic false teaching. Nor do I believe in "<u>one document copied perfectly for 1500 years.</u>" As I have said in many places above, Dr. Frederick Scrivener's Greek New Testament is an "*edition*" which made use primarily of Beza's 5th edition, 1598 in **99.86%** of the cases. In only 190 places out of the 140,521 Greek words (**0.14%**) did he use seven other non-English editions other than Beza's edition (See *Scrivener's Annotated Greek New Testament*, p. 648 as **BFT #1670 @ $35.00 + $7.50 S&H**). In so doing, Scrivener distilled the best of the Traditional, Received readings of former years. I believe that God kept His promise to preserve His Words and that he has done so in the Hebrew, Aramaic, and Greek Words underlying the King James Bible. I doubt that Sproul believes God made that promise, and if so, he doesn't know exactly where He has fulfilled it. So why is he so outraged with us who believe what we believe?

Don't Trust the Septuagint

STATEMENT #90. (p. 86) "*Will the majority of manuscripts, or maybe the oldest manuscripts, make this decision? Maybe the Bible used by <u>the earliest Christians, (Septuagint)</u> will be the deciding factor, or a text or version used for a long time, whether Septuagint, KJV, or TR?*"

COMMENT #90. Sproul raises a number of rhetorical and speculative questions. But he erroneously claims that "<u>the earliest Christians</u>" used the "*Septuagint.*" Though it is granted that a few Old Testament books were translated from Hebrew to Greek, there is no tangible proof that the entire Old Testament was available until the time of Origen (c. 185--254 A.D.). It was first found, not B.C., but A.D. in the fifth column of Origen's Hexapla which contained six columns as follows:

1. Hebrew
2. Hebrew transliterated into Greek characters
3. Aquila of Sinope
4. Symmachus the Ebionite
5. Septuagint
6. Theodotian (from *Wikipedia*, under *Hexapla*)

The early church used the Hebrew Old Testament because they were Jews who knew the Hebrew language.

Words "Inspired" Not People

STATEMENT #91. (p. 86, and footnote #11) Under the section of "*Apocrypha*," Sproul wrote: "*The autographs are Greek copies of the original New Testament and the Hebrew and Aramaic copies of the original Old Testament.*" In footnote #11, Sproul wrote: "*Unless one is a Ruckmanite, and simply believes God inspired the KJV translators as he did the original authors.*"

COMMENT #91. I am strongly anti-Ruckmanite and I believe it is rank heresy to say "*God inspired the KJV translators.*" Likewise I believe it is rank heresy for Sproul to imply that "*God inspired . . . the original authors.*" According to the Bible in 2 Timothy 3:16, God never "*inspired*" or "*breathed out*" any person in the whole world, including every Old Testament and New Testament writer. **God breathed out His Words, He did not breathe out people**. A second rank heresy in Sproul's statement is saying that the **writers** of the Old and New Testaments were "*authors*." An "*author*" has been defined as "*a person who makes or originates something; creator; originator.*" He is guilty of another rank heresy and indeed even blasphemy by saying that the Bible **writers** were really "*authors*" who "*originated or created*" the Words of the Bible rather than our God who was the only Author.

KJB Founded on "Majority of Witnesses"

STATEMENT #92. (p. 91) "*Because the 'KJV-Only' position rejects ancient witnesses (Alexandrian text) and the majority of witnesses (Majority text), its only rationale or existence is 'what we have always used must be the perfect one.'*"

COMMENT #92. Again, I reject the "*KJV-only*" smear Ruckmanite label which combines them with those like me who take a sound, sane, and sensible position on Bible texts and translations. I also reject the Alexandrian Gnostic text of the Vatican and Sinai manuscripts for good and sound reasons. Why shouldn't these false manuscripts be rejected since they are in gross doctrinal and verbal errors? I do not reject the "*majority of witnesses*" at all, but do not confine myself to the mere 414 witnesses of Von Soden on which the so-called "*Majority text*" is founded. How about 5,210 or so manuscripts for a real "Majority"!

STATEMENT #93. (pp. 91-92) "*If other godly Christians have not used the TR or if no proof exists for a 'secret' line in the Alps to preserve the TR, then the 'KJV-only' position loses any plausible rationale for its existence, unless it accepts Ruckman's double inspiration of the 1611 translators. If it does that, then fundamentalism is spared fanciful re-writes of history. KJV-onlyism already rejects as flawed the majority of witnesses and the most ancient witnesses. That must explain why a minority of recent witnesses is a more powerful testimony to*" *the text than either the majority of manuscripts or the most ancient manuscripts. This is a major conundrum of the 'KJV-only' position."*

COMMENT #93. That is a long quotation, but I certainly differ with Sproul's analysis here. First of all, the text that underlies the King James Bible was not a "*fanciful re-write of history.*" It is translated from Beza's 5ᵗʰ Edition of 1598. Secondly, the text that underlies our King James Bible is not supported by a minority of manuscripts. The text that underlies our King James Bible is in the majority of witnesses. **99.86%** of the manuscripts (5,210 out of 5,255) that we possessed as of 1967 are the Words that underlie our King James Bible. Kurt Aland as of 1967 had copies of 5,255 preserved manuscripts. Several hundred more have been found since then. Of the 5,255, only 45 are of the critical text variety (only Vatican "B" and Sinai "Aleph" and 43 others.) This is only **0.14%** of the evidence. The rest of the manuscripts (5,210 or **99.86%**) are of the traditional text variety. These are the ones underlying our King James Bible.

Sproul says we are throwing away the most ancient witnesses by which he means the Vatican and Sinai ("B" and "Aleph") manuscripts which he calls "*the most ancient witnesses.*" They came from Alexandra, Egypt, which was the educational center of Gnosticism's heresies. It is a known and a documented fact that many of these Gnostic heretics added to, subtracted from, or changed in other ways the original Words of the New Testament. The Vatican and Sinai manuscripts from Alexandria, Egypt are specimens of such alterations. No wonder I reject them. I reject them just as the early church rejected them. The early church considered these manuscripts to be in serious error. For this reason these manuscripts, from about 600 A.D. to the present, have not been re-copied. Therefore, these manuscripts and the so-called critical text have no continuity. They have no continuous history as the Textus Receptus has from Apostolic times to the present. **I reject the Vatican and Sinai manuscripts and their kin because they are the worse manuscripts of all.**

KJB's "Masoretic Text" Is "Inerrant"

STATEMENT #94. (p. 96, footnote #28) *"If the Masoretic Text as represented in Blainey's 1769 revision that Christians use today is the inerrant, 'exact' and infallible Word of God, then Timothy did not have that Bible."*

COMMENT #94. Timothy had the Hebrew Words that were preserved from when they were written. They are the same preserved Hebrew Words that the Lord Jesus Christ had and never once corrected. Our Saviour had no problems with these Words. He did not correct them or change them. He is the One who authored them. He, through God the Holy Spirit, gave every one of those Words, and the writers wrote them down. They are the same Hebrew Words that underlie the King James Bible.

Sproul's statement is unfounded and ridiculous.

No "Double Inspiration"

STATEMENT #95. (p. 96) Quoting one of Dr. Jeffrey Khoo's articles, Sproul wrote: *"'However, God "providentially guided" the KJV translators to exactly the right choice in Greek words as they translated into English' . . . Whether Khoo realizes it or not, he is arguing for double inspiration or on-going revelation for the KJV translators."*

COMMENT #95. Dr. Jeffrey Khoo is the Dean of the Far Eastern Bible College in Singapore. He most certainly does not believe in "*double inspiration*." Sproul has falsely charged Dr. Khoo in this. Dr. Khoo is very strongly opposed to the Peter Ruckman position that the King James Bible has been "*given by inspiration*." By no means is being *"providentially guided"* believing in "*double inspiration*."

Timothy Used the Hebrew O.T.

STATEMENT #96. (p. 96) *"Would those of the 'KJV-only' persuasion separate from Timothy and Paul because they use the Greek translation of the OT that is different from the Hebrew Masoretic Text."*

COMMENT #96. In the first place, there was no "*Greek translation of the OT*" in the days of Timothy and Paul. Though a few books were translated from Hebrew to Greek in the Old Testament, the entire Septuagint did not come into existence until Origen's days in around 225 A.D. Second, when the Lord Jesus Christ, the Author of every Old Testament Word wished to alter the Hebrew Words, that was within the Author's prerogative to make the point for which He was citing the verses.

No "Perfection" In Any Translation

STATEMENT #97. (p. 96, footnote #29) *"The argument of a 'special history' through the Waldenses by Moorman, Wilkinson, and Sorenson or Khoo's argument of 'dynamic preservation' are attempts to bypass the thorny problem faced by those who want to enshrine perfection on Blainey's 1769 revision or its predecessor, the 1611."*

COMMENT #97. We do not have a "*special history*." The Waldenses did use the Received Text. The Waldenses' Bible both in the early 2nd Century and the later centuries did use the text that underlies the King James Bible. So the Waldenses' Bible was an accurate picture of the history of translations from the right New Testament Greek Words and text.

The "LXX" Was A.D., Not B.C.

STATEMENT #98. (p. 97) He is quoting with approval Jerry Jarman: *"While the <u>Scripture writers</u> demonstrated a <u>decided preference</u> for <u>the readings of the LXX</u>, it must be noted that . . . "*

COMMENT #98. This is false. See my comment under **COMMENT #90** for the A.D. rather than the B.C. origin of the LXX (Septuagint.) The "<u>Scripture writers</u>" could not have a "<u>decided preference</u>" for something not in existence.

STATEMENT #99. (p. 98, footnote #14) Quoting with approval F. F. Bruce, Sproul wrote: *"The Septuagint was likely written about 200 B.C."*

COMMENT #99. This is absolutely false again. It was written in a little after 200 A.D. rather than 200 B.C. That is 400 years later. There is no ironclad proof that the Septuagint was written in 200 B.C. This is guesswork on the part of many. Sproul then quotes from the *Letter of Aristeas*, which is a false Apocryphal book.

> *"The so-called **Letter of Aristeas** is a pseudepigraphical Hellenstic work. Josephus (Antiquities XII:ii passim) ascribes to Aristeas a letter, written to Philocrates, describing the Greek translation of the Jewish Law to seventy-two interpreters sent into Egypt from Jerusalem at the request of the librarian of Alexandria, resulting in the Septuagint translation."* (From *Wikipedia*)

Even in the *Letter of Aristeas* it says these Jews only translated the Pentateuch or the first five books of Moses. There is nothing, even in the spurious and fictional *Letter of Aristeas* about the translation of the entire Old Testament. See my **COMMENT #90** above for the A.D. origin of the Septuagint.

STATEMENT #100. (p. 99) Sproul quoted with approval four alleged statements by the KJV translators from their Preface of the King James Bible:

1. *The KJV translators believed the Septuagint (LXX) existed before Christ.*
2. *The KJV translators believed the Septuagint was the apostles' Bible.*
3. *The KJV translators believed the Septuagint with all its problems was preferable for the New Testament church to a 'perfect' new translation because of the environment of the Early church.*
4. *The KJV translators believed that the Septuagint was God's Word even though the LXX was not perfect."*

COMMENT #100. If Sproul accurately quoted the beliefs of what the King James translators believed, then they were wrong. It is interesting that though Sproul has many questions on the King James Bible, he quotes the translators when it suits his purpose. I believe the translators were misled on the Septuagint in the same way as Sproul and others are. Standing for the King James Bible does not mean that I must agree with all of their beliefs in other areas. For instance, they were Anglicans, I am a Baptist. As such, there are many differences in our doctrines. The King James translators were skilled in translation and produced a good product in the King James Bible.

STATEMENT #101. (p. 100) Sproul quoted Dr. Edward F. Hills with approval: "*God had brought into being the Septuagint, the Greek Old Testament translation, which was to serve the Church as a temporary substitute until such a time as the ancient Hebrew Bible could be restored to her.*"

COMMENT #101. Dr. Edward Hills has a good book on the King James Bible, but I disagree with him as well on the subject of the Septuagint. He has a good book defending the Textus Receptus and the King James Bible, but since he was a Presbyterian and I am a Baptist, there are some differences in doctrines contained therein. Again, it is interesting that Sproul quotes Hills when it suits his purpose, but despises his defense of the TR and KJB.

STATEMENT #102. (p. 101) With approval, Sproul quoted Douglas Kutilek when he wrote: "*Dean John William Burgon (1813-1888), also clearly accepted a pre-Christian date for the Septuagint, . . .*"

COMMENT #102. Though I am in agreement that some parts of the Old Testament were translated from the Hebrew into the Greek, but not the whole Bible until the Hexapla of Origen who lived (c. 185--254 A.D.). I am in agreement with Dean Burgon on most of his views on Biblical matters, but do not think he was well informed on this subject (if Kutilek is really quoting Dean Burgon accurately). This was the prevailing opinion in Burgon's day.

STATEMENT #103. (p. 102) Sproul quotes Bruce Metzger's opinion that "*the Septuagint was the Bible of the early Christian Church. . .*"

COMMENT #103. That is another false statement. I certainly do not have to agree with Metzger. He was an apostate, an unbeliever, and in favor of the erroneous Critical Greek Text.

STATEMENT #104. (p. 102) Sproul is, no doubt, referring to the spurious and fictional *Letter of Aristeas* (mentioned above in my **COMMENT #99**) when he wrote: "*After the Greek-speaking Jews of Alexandria translated the Hebrew into Greek (about two hundred years before Christ), other people began translating the Greek Septuagint into the Old Latin, Coptic, Gothic . . .*"

COMMENT #104. I do not agree with that statement either. As I said, the *Letter of Aristeas* says that these "*Jews of Alexandria*" translated from Hebrew to Greek only the first five books of the Old Testament, and not the entire thirty-nine books. Therefore, this so-called Septuagint could not have been the basis for these other language translations. Once again, no one has ever been able to produce as evidence, in the B.C. time-frame, the entire thirty-nine books in Greek. This has only been accomplished in the A.D. time of Origen in his *Hexapla*.

"Preservation" In Original Languages

STATEMENT #105. (p. 102) "*Did God not promise perfect preservation to every generation of every word? According to many in the 'KJV-only' movement if one does not believe every word in the 1769 KJV (which uses the Masoretic Text) is identical to the original of Moses, then God has lied to believers concerning preservation.*"

COMMENT #105. In the first place, Sproul wants to throw me and others like me into this Ruckmanite spurious term of "*KJV-only.*" What he should have written was that the Ruckmanites believe this, but he chose to smear all of us who stand for the KJB. I don't even think that Peter Ruckman himself believes that "*every word in the 1769 KJV (which uses the Masoretic Text) is identical to the original of Moses.*" This is ridiculous on its face. How can Hebrew be "*identical*" to Hebrew in every respect? For me, and those who follow my understanding,

> "*Preservation,*" in the capital "P" sense, applies solely to the original Hebrew, Aramaic, and Greek Words.

"Septuagint" Wholly Unreliable

STATEMENT #106. (p. 103) Referring to some of the foreign language translations: "*. . . they also have the Septuagint and not the Masoretic Text as the underlying text behind the translation of the Old Testament.*"

COMMENT #106. This again is false. As I have said repeatedly above, Sproul cannot show me, or anyone else, a complete Septuagint which originated B.C. The LXX is an A.D. production by Origin.

TR MSS Not In "Extreme Minority"

STATEMENT #107. (p. 103, footnote #52) "*The TR is derived from an extreme minority of late manuscripts.*"

COMMENT #107. This is flagrantly false. The Textus Receptus is derived from **99.86%** of manuscripts that had been preserved and in the hands of Kurt Aland as of 1967. Of the 5,255 manuscripts at that time, 5,210 are manuscripts that underlie our King James Bible. That is **99.86%** of all the preserved manuscripts to that date. The other text comprises only 45 manuscripts or **0.14%** of the evidence. Dr. Jack Moorman's new 722-large-page volume bears this out. It is called *A Manuscript Digest of the New Testament--Preliminary Edition*. It is **BFT #3324** @ $40.00 + $8.00 S&H. It shows the tremendous number of manuscripts and other documentary evidence for each of the over 8,000 differences between the TR and the Critical Text. Dr. Moorman's hardback 544-page hardback book is available as **BFT #3084** @ $20.00 + $7.00 S&H.

The "Septuagint" Is A.D., Not B.C.

STATEMENT #108. (p. 110) *"Do modern scholars have copies of the Septuagint that date before Christ or to the time of Christ? Yes, they do."*

> **COMMENT #108.** That is a false statement. Sproul's so-called "scholars" do not have the complete Old Testament from Genesis through Malachi before the time of Christ. They have a few books, but not the complete Old Testament. Let's get honest here! The only complete Old Testament Septuagint is found in Origen's Hexapla which dates in the 200's A.D., not in the 200's B.C.

STATEMENT #109. (p. 111) *"This historic fact of the Essenes possessing the LXX is another nail in the coffin of the 'KJV-only' history concerning the Septuagint."*

COMMENT #109. Though Sproul seems to think it does, repetition of a false statement does not turn it into a true statement. The Essenes, from the second century B.C. and onward (*Wikipedia* article), did not possess the Septuagint Genesis through Malachi because it didn't exist. They have never produced a B.C. copy, nor can they. This cannot be proved.

Christ Did Not Quote From the LXX

STATEMENT #110. (p. 112) *"If Christ or the apostles sighted a less than absolutely perfect version (LXX), then why are some people today attacking and angrily separating from their brothers and sisters in Christ who use a modern version (NKJV) that does translate from the Masoretic Text and, therefore, is closer to the original, by 'KJV-only' standards than a version used by Christ and the apostles."*

COMMENT #110. There is so much falsity in this statement. The most important point is the Septuagint was not the text used by the Apostles and by Christ. We have an entire book that has been written entitled *Did Christ and the Apostles Quote from the Septuagint?* The author of that is Dr. Kirk DeVietro. If you are interested in reading this let us know. Since the Septuagint (LXX) was A.D., and not B.C., if there was any quoting from one source to the other, it would have to be the LXX quoting from Christ and the apostles rather than the reverse.

> As for the New King James Version, I found over 2,000 examples of this version using dynamic equivalency, that is, either adding to, subtracting from, or changing in other ways the Hebrew, Aramaic, or Greek Words. The report is available as BFT #1442 @ $10.00 + $7.00 S&H. This report gives over 2,000 reasons why the NKJV is unfaithful to the preserved

Hebrew, Aramaic, and Greek Words.

LXX Was A.D., Not B.C.

STATEMENT #111. (p. 114) *"Has Christianity ever debated <u>a version</u> <u>that is accepted as inerrant because of longevity of usage</u>. Now that it is clear that the LXX <u>predates Christ</u>, other applications to the '<u>KJV-only</u>' discussion can be asserted."*

COMMENT #111. By Sproul's repetition that the Septuagint "*<u>predates Christ</u>*" doesn't make it so. He repeats this over an over. Let him tell me and others of the location of the 200 B.C. entire Old Testament from Genesis through Malachi in the Greek language. He has never done this, nor can he or others of his persuasion. After he has told me where this document is located, I can see if I can take a look at it. Is it in Sproul's basement, perhaps? Sproul's question brings up "<u>*a version that is accepted as inerrant because of longevity of usage*</u>." He assumes that this is a "*<u>KJV-only</u>*" of all of us who stand for the King James Bible whereas it is limited to the followers of Peter Ruckman.

As I have said before, I do not use the term "*<u>inerrant</u>*" for any "*<u>version</u>*," but only for the original preserved Words of Hebrew, Aramaic, and Greek underlying the King James Bible.

STATEMENT #112. (p. 114) *"... if the Septuagint has been translated in A.D. 200 as Ruckman and some others in the 'KJV-only' group would like their followers to believe, then Augustine has no reason to argue that the church has 'always' had the Septuagint."*

COMMENT #112. In the first place, Sproul includes "*Ruckman*" in the "*KJV-only*" group.

In fact, "*KJV-only*" is Sproul's favorite smear term for all of us who use and defend the King James Bible despite the fact that we are strongly anti-Ruckman in our views of that Bible.

The lack of evidence for a complete Old Testament in Greek before the time of Origen in the A.D. 200's does not rest on whether or not it is believed by Peter Ruckman. Augustine was only repeating the false line taught in his day about the so-called B.C. Septuagint. He was in error along with the many others Sproul has adduced.

KJB Not Based on "Erasmus"

STATEMENT #113. (pp. 117-118) Sproul spoke of the first edition of the Erasmus Greek New Testament: *". . . but even a strong defender of the Traditional Text like Scrivener claimed Erasmus' 'first' TR was extremely 'faulty' because of the speed in which Erasmus produced it."*

COMMENT #113. So "*Erasmus' first TR*" was "*faulty.*" So what! There were many spellings in the 1516 edition that had to be corrected. The implication is that the King James Bible used the Erasmus' 1516 first edition as its base. This implication is completely false. The King James translators chose to take the 5th edition of Beza of 1598 as a base. This was 82 years after Erasmus' edition of 1516 where these various details were cared for.

There Is No "Inspired KJV"

STATEMENT #114. (p. 121, footnote #101) "*To be consistent with their view of an inspired KJV they must criticize the accepted Bible' of the Spanish world.*"

COMMENT #114. I do not believe that any translation is "*inspired*" or God-breathed, including the King James Bible. This is Ruckman or semi-Ruckman terminology.

> The term for "*given by inspiration of God*" in 2 Timothy 3:16 is THEOPNEUSTOS which means, literally, "*God-breathed.*" The only Words that were "*breathed out by God*" were in the original Hebrew, Aramaic, and Greek languages and no other languages

Sproul doesn't give the date of the Spanish Bible, but he probably means the Spanish Bible of 1960. That Bible is based on the false Critical Greek text of Westcott and Hort and others. This is why Dr. Humberto Gomez has worked hundreds of hours on his Spanish Bible to conform it to the Masoretic Hebrew Text and to the Textus Receptus which underlies our King James Bible. It is now available as **BFT #3257/L @ $25.00 + S&H** for leather and **BFT #3257/HB @ $15.00 + S&H** for hardback.

"Perfect Preservation" of Copies

STATEMENT #115. (p. 122) "*What passages cause difficulty for the 'perfect preservation of the KJV translation' view? Are there word differences that change meanings between 1611 and 1769?*"

> **COMMENT #115.** I do not believe in the "*perfect preservation of the KJV translation.*" I believe rather in the verbal plenary preservation of the original Hebrew, Aramaic, and Greek Words that underlie the King James Bible. Because of its accurate translation methods, I believe the King James Bible "*preserves*" (with a small "p") in English the "*Preserved*" (with a capital "P") original Hebrew, Aramaic, and Greek Words underlying the King James Bible. It is obvious that the original 1611 King James Bible has gone through several editions and is, therefore, not itself "*perfectly preserved*" in that sense. However, there are relatively few minor differences between the 1611 and the 1769 edition of the King James Bible that we use today.

STATEMENT #116. (p. 125) *"God's method and definition of preservation might be different than those of the 'KJV-only' persuasion prefer, but God never lies. KJV-onlyism might misinterpret or misunderstand God's Word, but God never lies."*

COMMENT #116. It is true that God never lies, but why does Sproul suggest that "*KJV-onlyism might misinterpret or misunderstand God's Word*"? As I have said repeatedly, **I disdain the smear term, "KJV-only,"** which includes the Ruckmanite heretics. I and those who agree with me do not either "*misinterpret or misunderstand God's Word.*" I believe God promised to preserve His original Hebrew, Aramaic, and Greek Words and He has done so in the Words underlying the King James Bible. Sproul believes God only promised to preserve His "*Word*" which means to him and his followers only the "*ideas, thoughts, concepts, message, truth, or teachings,*" but not God's "*Words.*" It is Sproul and his followers who "*misinterpret or misunderstand God's Word.*"

STATEMENT #117. (p. 125) *"If an individual today has the 'perfect' Bible then those Christians of 1611 did not have it because word changes in Blainey's revision have affected meaning."*

COMMENT #117. The "*perfect Bible*" that Sproul refers **to is not the King James Bible, but the Hebrew, Aramaic, and Greek Words underlying the King James Bible that are "*perfect.*"** They are the same Words that we have today and have not undergone any "*revision*" by Blayney or anyone else. So what is Sproul's problem?

False "Doctrine" Is Involved In MSS

STATEMENT #118. (p. 125) *"the word differences among all Greek and Hebrew manuscripts are minor and do not affect any doctrine that is not taught somewhere else."*

COMMENT #118. That is one of the biggest lies Sproul has told yet. I am limiting my comments to the Greek manuscripts for now.

First of all, the "*word differences*" in the Greek New Testament are huge. They are "*major*" and not "*minor*" at all. Dr. Jack Moorman has documented over *8,000 Differences between the Textus Receptus of the King James Bible and the Critical Text*. See his 525-page hardback book as BFT #3084 @ $20.00 + $7.00 S&H for all 8,000 differences from Matthew through Revelation.

Dr. Moorman has recently followed up this hardback book with another more detailed study entitled *A Manuscript Digest of the New Testament--A Preliminary Edition*. This 722-large-page report can be received as **BFT #3325 for a gift of $40.00 + $8.00 S&H.** Documented manuscript and other authority is given for each of these 8,000 differences.

> Secondly, these more than 8,000 differences account for 356 doctrinal passages that are erroneous in the Critical Text. These can be found on pages 119 to 312 of the 456-page hardback book by Dr. Jack Moorman. It is called *Early Manuscripts, Church Fathers, and the Authorized Version* (BFT #3230 @ $20.00 + $7.00 S&H). Of these 356, there are many that are taught in no other place. Even if some of them might be found elsewhere, they should be included in every place where they belong. Sproul doesn't know what he is talking about in these matters. He should get all three of these above books and correct his falsehoods.

KJB "Accurate," Not "Perfect"

STATEMENT #119. (p. 126) *"KJV-onlyism reports that if one cannot know every word in the King James 1769 revision of the Bible is <u>perfect</u>, then one can never identify any word as true."*

COMMENT #119. As I have mentioned before, I do not use the term "<u>perfect</u>" for anything that man has done. I use the word "*accurate*" for the King James Bible's translation. Since this is true, I do not have to answer Sproul's ridiculous proposition.

How God's "Words" Are Preserved

STATEMENT #120. (p. 126) *"Yet in the discussion of <u>preservation</u>, a middle option does exist: the tremendously <u>preserved Word of God</u> has in each <u>version</u> in every language of the Bible 'mistakes of less moment,' but these mistakes do not mean that individuals do not <u>have God's Word today</u>. Christians have all the information they need in every version. . . ."*

COMMENT #120. Sproul's discussion of "*preservation*" is totally off base.

> Biblical preservation does not primarily concern translations. It deals with the status of the original Hebrew, Aramaic, and Greek Words.

Sproul uses the words "<u>*preserved Word of God*</u>" and "<u>*have God's Word today*</u>" to indicate that he does not believe in the "*preservation*" of the original Hebrew, Aramaic, and Greek Words, but only in the "*ideas, thoughts, concepts, message, truth, or teachings*" of the Bible. These two views are poles apart. Sproul's view is erroneous, unbiblical, and even heretical. It denies the Lord Jesus Christ's preservation promises (Matthew 5:18; 24:35; Mark 13:31; Luke 21:33).

King James Bible Is the Best of All

STATEMENT #121. (p. 126) *". . . some versions are clearly <u>better than others</u> . . ."*

COMMENT #121. This is true. But why settle for "*better than others*" when you can have the King James Bible which is the "*best of all*" in the English language. Every other English translation adds to God's Words, subtracts from God's Words, or changes God's Words in some other way.

Hebrew "Vowel Points" Were Original

STATEMENT #122. (p. 133) Speaking of the Hebrew Old Testament text, Sproul wrote: "*The Masoretes added vowel points to the text around 500 to 950 A.D.*"

COMMENT #122. Dr. Thomas Strouse, the Dean of Emmanuel Baptist Theological Seminary in Newington, Connecticut, has written an excellent paper regarding the vowel points in the Hebrew Old Testament. He shows that the vowels in the Hebrew Bible were in the originals. It is *called A Dissertation on the Hebrew Vowel-Points* (BFT #3327 @ $2.00 + $1.00 S&H.) The Hebrew Words could not be Words unless they have vowels. It cannot be a Hebrew Word without vowels.

> To say, as Sproul says, that the vowel points did not come into existence until "*500 to 950 A.D.*," is to say we never had an accurate and real Bible with real and specific Words in it until *500 to 950 A.D.* So, the people were without the accurate Words of God until these years.

This is totally false. I used to believe this. I was taught this. As a matter of fact, this was in the first nine editions of my book, *Defending the King James Bible*. I changed it in the tenth edition. I was taught this at Dallas Theological Seminary by the Hebrew professor, Dr. Merrill F. Unger. Dr. Strouse lists a number of illustrations. If you do not have the vowels in Hebrew, you can have all kinds of different words rather than the true Words of God in the Old Testament. We would never know what Words were real and what Words were not real. Dr. Strouse shows very clearly that these vowels were part of the original Hebrew text.

No "Inspiration" of Translators

STATEMENT #123. (p. 133) "*If this double inspiration of translators is accurate then why did God not inspire the Masoretic and Septuagint translators to put both Words.*"

COMMENT #123. This is a repeat of Sproul's error mentioned in **STATEMENT #5** where he referred to "*apostles and prophets whom the Holy Spirit inspired.*" God did not inspire any man. God breathed out **WORDS**, not men. God did not "*inspire*" translators of any sort. To believe that God "*breathes out men*" or "*inspires men*" is a serious doctrinal heresy. By his misuse of the term "*inspired*" and "*inspiration*," it shows that Sproul is ignorant of the important and vital Biblical doctrine of inspiration. Because of this ignorance, Sproul has made many other serious errors in his book dealing with this book entitled *God's Word Preserved.*

Doctrine Is Seriously Affected

STATEMENT #124. (p. 133) "T*he correct answer is this is a difference of "less moment" that does not affect one doctrine.*"

COMMENT #124. Though Sproul is referring to an Old Testament "*difference*," he implants the notion that a "*difference*" even in the Greek New Testament "*does not affect one doctrine.*"

> On the contrary, in the New Testament Greek text there are 356 passages that affect 356 "*doctrines.*"

This is found on pages 119 to 312 in *Early Manuscripts, Church Fathers, and the Authorized Version* (BFT #3230 @ $20.00 + $7.00 S&H) by Dr. Jack Moorman.

"Greek Septuagint" Not "Inspired"

STATEMENT #125. (p. 133) Sproul comments on differences between the Hebrew Old Testament and the Greek Septuagint translation of the Old Testament: *"However, this difference effectively eliminates the 'KJV-only' position that the Greek TR of Scrivener and the Masoretic Text are the 'exact' words of the autographs because these two texts use different words to explain the same events."*

COMMENT #125. Obviously Sproul, whose book title is *God's **Word** Preserved*, does not believe that "*God's **Words** were preserved*" and makes fun of those of us who do! He just believes that only the *"ideas, thoughts, concepts, message, truth, or teachings,"* were "*preserved.*" This is no real preservation at all! If the Hebrew Old Testament differs at any time from the A.D. Septuagint, the Hebrew alone must be followed, not the erroneous Septuagint. It is as simple as that.

No KJB "Double Inspiration"

STATEMENT #126. (p. 138) In the Summary, *"The 'KJV-only' position of accepting either one perfect document passed from one 'good guy' to another for hundreds of years in the meantime and in caves of Europe, or a **double inspiration view of the King James translators' product that believes the Holy Sprit guided the 1611 translators to select certain words or phrases** that do not have any Greek or Hebrew manuscript support and claim these Latin words as 'exactly' the words of the autographs should cause any Separatist, Evangelical pastor, or layman grave concern about the 'KJV-only' interpretation of Scripture and history."*

COMMENT #126. Here is Sproul's Ruckmanite smear once again of all of us anti-Ruckmanites.

> The King James Bible translators did not have a Ruckmanite "*double inspiration*" to give them God's Words in English. They had God-breathed Words preserved for them in Hebrew, Aramaic, and Greek, and they gave an accurate translation of those Words into the English language.

I deny strongly Sproul's repeated lie that the King James translators "*created*" the Textus Receptus. They simply translated the Textus Receptus in hand.

STATEMENT #127. (p. 118) "*Asserting perfection for the TR or Masoretic text underlying the KJV, rather than the KJV itself, does not avoid the charge of Ruckmanism or double inspiration. The KJV translators created the TR underlying the KJV when they translated the KJV.*"

COMMENT #127. I, and many others like me, believe in the verbal, plenary preservation of the Hebrew, Aramaic, and Greek Words underlying the King James Bible and completely deny any Ruckmanistic "*double inspiration*" which Sproul falsely charges. When Sproul wrote that the "*KJV translators created the TR underlying the KJV,*" he is once again twisting facts and showing his bias for smear and falsehood of those with whom he disagrees. As I have said before, the King James translators held Beza's 5th edition of 1598 in their hands which they did not "*create.*" According to Dr. Frederick Scrivener, they used that edition 99.86% of the time. In only 190 places did they use some documents other than Beza's 5th edition. Since there are 140,521 Greek Words in the New Testament, 190 places would only amount to 0.14% places that varied from Beza's Greek edition. The translators did not "*create*" anything. They followed an edition that was already in print. Why does Sproul persist in lying about this matter?

No KJB Translators' "Inspiration"

STATEMENT #128. (p. 118) "*Therefore, if some claim to believe in the perfection of the TR that underlies the King James Version, these people believe in the inspiration of the KJV translators just as much as Ruckman does,* ..."

COMMENT #128. When Sproul says "*these people believe in the inspiration of the KJV translators,*" he is again spouting lying falsehood. His heresy regarding "inspiration" is continuously repeated throughout this book. God's "inspiration," (THEOPNEUSTOS) according to the Bible (2 Timothy 3:16) is confined to His breathing out of His Words. God has never "*breathed out*" men, including the "*KJV translators.*" No man can be "*inspired.*" Only words can be "*inspired.*"

CHAPTER FOUR: GOD'S COMMUNICATION THROUGH THE MULTITUDE OF COUNSELORS (pp. 141-207)

"Words" Not "Word" Preservation

STATEMENT #129. (Chapter 4, p. 139) The title and subtitle of this Chapter is: *"God's Communication Through the Multitude of Counselors--The Historical Beliefs of Evangelicals, Separatists and Baptists Concerning the Communication, Transmission and **Preservation of God's Word**."*

COMMENT #129. When he uses the term, the "**Preservation of God's Word**," he does not mean the "**Preservation of God's Words**." This is extremely deceptive. Normally, a person might think that "Word" and "Words" referred to the same thing, but not in Sproul's distorted definition. By "*Word*" of God, he means only the *"ideas, thoughts, concepts, message, truth, or teachings"* of God, but not His *"Words."* This is the only "*preservation*" Sproul believes in. This is a defective and heretical view of Bible "*preservation*."

No "Back-Translation" by Scrivener

STATEMENT #130. (p. 141) Sproul used this phrase: "*. . . after Scrivener back-translated the 1611 translators' choices in English into Greek . . .*"

COMMENT #130. This is absolutely false. Sproul has no evidence for this whatsoever. The Dean Burgon Society has reprinted Dr. Frederick Scrivener's Greek New Testament under the name of *Scrivener's Annotated Greek New Testament* (#1670 @ $35.00 + $7.00 S&H). It was not a back translation from English into Greek. Scrivener was asked by the Cambridge

University Press to publish the Greek text underlying the King James Bible with notation of the changes made in the Westcott and Hort Greek text and the 1881 English Revised Version. According to his own testimony, Scrivener's text is Beza's 5th edition of 1598 except for the 190 places he lists in his Appendix. As I explained earlier, there are 140,521 words in the Greek New Testament. 190 places would only amount to 0.14% places that varied from Beza's Greek edition. This would amount to the King James Bible's following of Beza's Greek edition 99.86% of the time.

There is no evidence from Sproul or anyone else that Dr. Scrivener "*back-translated*" anything!

KJB Translators Not "Immoral"

STATEMENT #131. (p. 145) "*. . . but the actual 'bad guys,' King James and many of the immoral translators of the KJV, receive favorable treatment as, 'good guys.'*"

COMMENT #131. Sproul's charge of '*immoral translators of the KJV*' is both unfounded and unjust. If Sproul really believes the King James Bible translators were "*immoral*," why does he preach from the KJB and why does he use it in his church's academy? One translator was unjustly accused of drinking on the job as he translated. This has been disproved. He began drinking after his translating task had been completed. He is smearing the entire group of the King James Bible translators with an untruth.

Not "All Translations" Are Pure

STATEMENT #132. (p. 154) Referring to Benjamin Keech's view of preservation, Sproul wrote: "*This is contained exactly and most purely in the Originals and in all Translations, so far as they agree therewith.*"

COMMENT #132. That is false. The Words of God are not contained purely "*in all Translations.*" There may be translations of the pure Words of God, but strictly speaking capital letter "P" for Preservation refers exclusively to the original Hebrew, Aramaic, and Greek Words, rather than any translations of those preserved Words. I believe God has Preserved His original Hebrew, Aramaic, and Greek Words which underlie the King James Bible. That is where "*exactly and most purely*" Bible preservation is to be found. I do not agree with Benjamin Keech's statement.

DBS Not A "KJV-only" Society

STATEMENT #133. (p. 174) Sproul is referring to Dean J. W. Burgon: "*In fact, a 'KJV-only' Society named after him publishes books and pamphlets on this subject. Does this 'KJV-only' Society agree with its 'namesake'?*"

COMMENT #133. Sproul calls the Dean Burgon Society (DBS) a _"'KJV-only' Society."_ I have said many times above that this epithet is a smear term seeking to tie its recipients with Peter Ruckman's heresies on the King James Bible. Because of this, I totally oppose this term. While we do not agree with all that Dean Burgon stands for, the Dean Burgon Society uses the name of Dean Burgon because of his stand for the traditional texts of the Old and New Testaments, his opposition to the Critical Text of Westcott and Hort, his opposition for the theory behind that text, his opposition to the English Revised Version, and his support for the King James Bible. On the bottom of our Dean Burgon Newsletters, we print the following:

> _"The Dean Burgon Society, Inc. proudly takes its name in honor of John William Burgon (1813-1888), the Dean of Chichester in England, whose tireless and accurate scholarship and contribution in the area of New Testament textual criticism; whose defense of the Greek Traditional New Testament Text against its many enemies; and whose firm belief in the verbal inspiration and inerrancy of the Bible; we believe have all been unsurpassed either before or since his time."_

That is what we believe and that is why we have taken his name. We don't have to believe everything that he believes. I am an independent Baptist. We have a man in the DBS who is a Bible Brethren. We have a few Bible Presbyterian men in the Dean Burgon Society. This is not a denominational society, it is a society that stands for one main theme, "IN DEFENSE OF TRADITIONAL BIBLE TEXTS."

Dean Burgon Would Not Cut DBS

STATEMENT #134. (p. 174) Sproul is speaking of Dean J. W. Burgon: _"Could he freely speak on the subject of **preservation** at a meeting of the Dean Burgon Society, or is it is more likely that his preference might be **to cut associational ties with D. A. Waite and the Dean Burgon Society**?"_

COMMENT #134. Dean Burgon believed that God promised to preserve His Hebrew, Aramaic, and Greek Words and gave many years of his adult life to find out where these Words were preserved. The Dean Burgon Society believes, as Dean Burgon, that the Old Testament Hebrew and Aramaic Words should not be _"tinkered."_ Until all of his requirements would be fulfilled, (which have never been fulfilled) he said the Textus Receptus as it now stands would never lead any critical student astray.

Based on this, the Dean Burgon Society stands for the Traditional Hebrew and the Traditional Greek Words. If Dean Burgon were still living, there would be no need for a Dean Burgon Society. Rather than "**to cut associational ties with D. A. Waite and the Dean Burgon Society**," I believe he would have some close fellowship with "*D. A. Waite and the Dean Burgon Society.*" I think he would feel honored to have such a society named for him.

DBS Is Anti-Ruckmanite

STATEMENT #135. (p. 174) Speaking of the Dean Burgon Society, Sproul said: "*The 'KJV-only' movement* is *transitioning from its founders' beliefs to Ruckman.*"

COMMENT #135. How can Sproul dare to label the Dean Burgon Society a "*'KJV-only' movement*!" We are not associated with this Ruckmanism smear term, but renounce Ruckmanism in all of its forms. Furthermore, how can Sproul say that the DBS is *transitioning from its founders' beliefs to Ruckman*? I was the one who conceived of the Dean Burgon Society, and along with Dr. David Otis Fuller and Pastor E. L. Bynum, called for the first meeting. I drafted the DBS Constitution and Articles of Faith. We three were the DBS "*founders*" and the DBS has never changed its "*beliefs.*" We are not "*transitioning . . . to Ruckman*" nor will we ever do so.

Original Words Are Preserved Words

STATEMENT #136. (p. 174) "*Yet, D. A. Waite, who is the President of the Dean Burgon Society wrote,*

'*It is my own personal conviction and belief, after studying the subject since 1971, that the words of the Received Greek and Masoretic Hebrew texts that underlie the King James Bible are the very* [Author's emphasis] *words which God has preserved down through the centuries, being the exact words of the originals themselves. As such, I believe they are inspired words. I believe they are preserved words. I believe they are inerrant words. I believe they are infallible words.*'"

COMMENT #136. That's exactly what I believe. This is a quote from *Defending the King James Bible* (pages 48 and 49). I have not changed my belief from this. How is that transitioning to Ruckmanism? This is not what Ruckman believes. He believes in the "*inspiration*" of the King James Bible which is a heresy. Ruckman is a "*false teacher*" and this is one of his many "*damnable heresies*" (2 Peter 2:1).

> What is the Old or New Testament original Words in which Sproul has total confidence? He hasn't anything but doubts and questions as to the very original Hebrew, Aramaic, and Greek Words God has preserved for us to this day.

Scrivener's TR--"Exact Words of God"

STATEMENT #137. (p. 175, footnote #99) Referring to my own belief which he quoted in **#136** above, Sproul asked: "*My question is, 'Which one of* *the many TRs has the "exact words of God?" Between Scrivener's 1881 that underlies the KJV and the 1550 TR published by Stephen exist multiply variants in Romans 8:11 alone."'*

COMMENT #137. Though I cannot prove my belief to anyone who does not want to accept it, I have defined what I believe to be the *"exact Words of God."* They are the Hebrew, Aramaic, and Greek Words underlying the King James Bible. For the New Testament I have explained that is Scrivener's Greek New Testament. Sproul has quoted my definition in **#136** above, and then asks where I believe the *"exact Words of God"* are. Is he incapable of understanding plain English?

Verbal, Plenary Preservation (VPP)

STATEMENT #138. (p. 180) Quoting Dr. Lewis Sperry Chafer, Sproul wrote: *"By **plenary** [emphasis his] inspiration is meant that the accuracy which verbal inspiration secures, is extended to every portion of the Bible . . . The claim for verbal, plenary inspiration is made only for the original writings and does not extend to any transcriptions or translations."*

COMMENT #138. Dr. Chafer, the founder of Dallas Theological Seminary, was my teacher at this seminary for the last four years of his life (1948-1952). Dr. Chafer was writing about *"verbal, plenary inspiration."* I believe in this. I also believe in the *"verbal, plenary preservation"* of the original Hebrew, Aramaic, and Greek Words.

An "Inerrant TR"

STATEMENT #139. (p. 198) Sproul asked *"Did the pro-KJV people historically believe in __an inerrant TR or KJV__?"* Sproul specifically asked if *"the men who wrote articles in __Which Bible?__ believed what the __current leaders of the 'KJV-only' movement believe,__ namely, that the TR Greek Text or Masoretic Hebrew Text and /or the KJV language version could claim the title of __'exact' reproduction of the original."__*

COMMENT #139. Sproul used the words, *__'exact' reproduction of the original,__* that I used in **#136** above. He is talking about me.

First, I have never said I believe in "__an inerrant KJV__." That is pure Ruckmanism. I do not say that the King James Bible or any other Bible is the exact reproduction of the originals because the King James Bible was written in English and the originals were written in Hebrew, Aramaic, and Greek.

I believe the Hebrew, Aramaic, and Greek Words underlying the King James Bible are "*inerrant*," not the King James Bible itself.

Second, I am not a "*current leader of the 'KJV-only' movement*." In fact, I am solidly opposed to this Ruckman smear term and decry such a movement.

Third, so what if these men did not believe in an "*inerrant TR*"? Are we to be bound by what others might or might not believe? I do not think so.

Textus Receptus—No"Clear Errors"

STATEMENT #140. (p. 199) He is quoting Alfred Martin, "*One cannot say that the **Textus Receptus**, for example, is **verbally inspired**. It contains many plain and clear errors, as all schools of textual critics agree.*"

COMMENT #140. I do not agree with Sproul or Martin on this at all. The original Greek Words were verbally and plenarily inspired by God. If the copies of those "*verbally inspired*" Words in the "*Textus Receptus*" are the same Words in the originals (as I believe the Greek Words underlying the King James Bible are), those Words are "*verbally inspired*" though they were not given by the **process** of inspiration, but are the **product** of inspiration by copying.

KJB Not "Inerrant or Infallible"

STATEMENT #141. (pp. 199-200) Sproul is quoting from Dr. David Otis Fuller. "*When, therefore, the great bulk of witnesses--in proportion suppose of 100 or even 50 to 1--yield unfaltering testimony to a certain reading, and the remaining little handful of authorities, while advocating a different reading are yet observed to be unable to agree among themselves as to what that different reading concerning which all that discrepancy of detail is observed to exist may be regarded as **certainly false**. . . . This influential book in the 'KJV-only' movement admits the TR is not **perfect** and by extension, that the KJV cannot be inerrant or infallible.*"

COMMENT #141. The first part of this statement is a good one. I do not say that the King James Bible is "*perfect, inerrant, or infallible.*" I do not use these words for anything that man does. Only God Himself is "*perfect, inerrant, or infallible.*" I use these words for the Hebrew, Aramaic, and Greek Words underlying the King James Bible.

"Translators" Did Not "Create" A TR

STATEMENT #142. (p. 200) "*Men like Cloud, Waite, and Khoo are clearly considered 'unreasonable' by Brown, Rice, or Martin, because Cloud, Waite and Khoo consider the TR and/or the 1611 English Version that the translators created as the 'exact' representation of the original documents.*"

COMMENT #142. First of all, I do not believe the "*1611 English Version*" to be the "*'exact' representation of the original documents.*" This is a heretical position. The "*original documents,*" for example, did not contain the Apocrypha, as did the "*1611 English Version.*"

Second, there is no "*TR . . . that the translators created.*" Sproul has no proof of this inane statement whatsoever. The translators followed (with only 190 exceptions) Beza's 5th edition of 1598. They did not "*create*" their own Greek text.

Third, I believe that the Hebrew, Aramaic, and Greek Words underlying the King James Bible are the "*'exact' representation of the original documents.*" This is what I have stated repeatedly as being my confident position by fact and by faith. Sproul doesn't know and has no confident faith in what the Words of the original documents were. He is a Biblical skeptic filled with uncertainty.

DBS Is Not Close to Ruckmanism

STATEMENT #143. (p. 200) Sproul's heading reads: "*Is the 'KJV-only' movement settled theologically?*" He then wrote, when talking about Dean John W. Burgon: "*However, while claiming him as their founder, the position of the Dean Burgon Society today is much closer to Peter Ruckman than it is to Dean Burgon.*"

COMMENT #143. This is one more of Sproul's blatant falsehoods and lies. I have been the President of the Dean Burgon Society (DBS) since its founding in 1978. I have repeatedly denounced the position of Peter Ruckman, and have made sure that none of his followers were in the DBS leadership. Several of them were present at the founding of the DBS and soon left. Others who were using the terminology of Ruckman that the King James Bible was "*inspired*" have also left the DBS leadership. The Dean Burgon Society has a strong anti-Ruckman stance and will remain so as long as I am its President.

"KJV-only"--Smear For Ruckmanites

STATEMENT #144. (p. 201) "*The 'KJV-only' followers and leaders want an exact Greek Textus Receptus.*"

COMMENT #144. Once again, I am not a "*KJV-only*" either follower or leader. This is a term for the Ruckmanites and does not characterize me or those who agree with me. But I certainly, not only, "*want an exact Greek Textus Receptus,*" but I have one with the Greek Words underlying the King James Bible.

I Am Not A "KJV-only" Advocate

STATEMENT #145. (p. 202) "*One of the two groups of people is deceived. Either Fundamentalism's godly Fathers, Richard Clearwaters, Bob Jones Sr., A. T. Robertson, D. L. Moody, Noel Smith, John R. Rice, Ernest Pickering, W. B. Riley, R. A. Torrey, James Gray, C. I. Scofield, et al., are wrong and deceived along with their heirs who hold their position on preservation, or*

'KJV-only' advocates D. A. Waite, David Cloud, Dell Johnson, Jeffrey Khoo, David Sorenson and their followers are fooled and in error."

    COMMENT #145. First, once again, I am not a "*'KJV-only' advocate*.

    Second, must the Bible-believing Christians living in the 21st Century be shackled by the beliefs of the so-called "*Fundamentalism's godly Fathers*" of the 20th Century if they are in error, no matter how many names are listed? I believe not. I believe the Biblical evidence must be the deciding factor rather than the beliefs of "*Fundamentalism's godly Fathers*."

    Third, what was "*their position on preservation*" of the Bible? Was it the deceptive position of Sproul and those who follow him that holds merely to the Bible "*preservation*" of only the "*Word*" of God, but not that of the original Hebrew, Aramaic, and Greek "*Words*" of God? And as I have written many times above, by "*Word*" of God, Sproul and his followers mean only the "*ideas, thoughts, concepts, message, truth, or teachings*" of God, but not His original Hebrew, Aramaic, and Greek "*Words*." This is no Bible "*preservation*" at all. It is rather a denial of it by clever and ingenious semantics.

    It is the "*godly Fathers*" who are wrong. It is the "*godly Fathers*" who are deceived. They were deceived in this area either because they never studied it out, or because they accepted the lies of Bishop Westcott and Professor Hort without question.

1769 Not "Perfect Preservation" Bible

    STATEMENT #146. (p. 203) Sproul speaks of "*many in the 'KJV-only' camp*" who believe in " *the perfect preservation of Blayney's 1769 revision of the 1611* . . .*the rhetoric, hyperbole, and harsh language, etc., all reveal this belief as a core to 'KJV-only.'*"

    COMMENT #146. Again, I am not in the "*'KJV-only' camp*." One of the reasons is their outlandish belief in the "*perfect preservation of Blayney's 1769 revision of the 1611*." By Sproul's putting me into this group, he is once again committing false witness. I do believe that the 1769 KJB is the only accurate translation of the verbally and plenarily preserved original Hebrew, Aramaic, and Greek Words underlying it.

"Translators" Did Not "Create" A TR

    STATEMENT #147. (p. 204) "*This view lands them in Ruckman's lap theologically because the KJV translators created by their English word choices a TR that was a brand new edition.*"

    COMMENT #147. Once again Sproul is repeating this blatant lie that the King James Bible translators "*created by their English word choices a TR that was a brand new edition*." They did not "*create . . . a TR*." They used Beza's 5th edition 1598. According to Dr. Frederick Scrivener, they used some other source in only 190 places which is only 0.14% of the Greek New Testament's words. Sproul offers no documentation for this TR creation by the KJB translators. It is ludicrous and inane. Does 0.14% of the Greek New Testament constitute a TR in Sproul's mind? 99.86% of the King James Bible's underlying Greek text is that of Beza's 5th edition of 1598.

Here are Dr. Scrivener's own words about the King James Bible's text. The quotation is taken from the Preface of *Scrivener's Annotated Greek New Testament*, pp. vii-viii (**BFT #1670 @ $35.00 + S&H**):

> *"Between 1598 and 1611 no important edition appeared; so that Beza's fifth and last text of 1598 was more likely than any other to be in the hands of the King James's revisors, and to be accepted by them as the best standard within their reach. It is moreover found on comparison to agree more closely with the Authorised Version than any other Greek text; and accordingly it has been adopted by the Cambridge Press as the primary authority; . . ."*

No "Double Inspiration"

STATEMENT #148. (p. 204) *"Therefore, when they insist that when the TR behind the KJV contains the 'exact' words of Paul or Matthew, ipso facto, they are claiming double inspiration for the translators' product."*

COMMENT #148. It is a blatant lie for Sproul to say of me and others who agree that "*they are claiming double inspiration for the translators' product.*" Nothing could be further from the truth. I do not believe this. This is one of the slanderous errors of Sproul by putting me and others into the "KJV-only" Ruckman category. This is a Peter Ruckmanite doctrine of "*double inspiration.*" He teaches that the words of the King James Bible were "*inspired*" (which means "*God-breathed*") and thus were "*advanced revelation*" and often "*corrected*" the underlying Hebrew, Aramaic, and Greek Words. This is pure heresy! I do not believe this in any way, shape or form.

I Am Not A "KJV-only" Advocate

STATEMENT #149. (p. 204) *"This chapter demonstrates that the 'KJV-only' movement is in flux. Even writers in Which Bible do not agree with many of the current 'KJV-only' advocates."*

COMMENT #149. Again, let me repeat, I am not a "*'KJV-only' advocate.*" When Sproul puts me and others who totally disagree with the Ruckmanite followers into this "*KJV-only*" category, he is knowingly and purposely unfair, lying, falsifying, unreasonable, illogical, unchristian, smearing, unethical, disgraceful, and untruthful. I resent vehemently Sproul's doing this!

No "Borrowing" From Peter Ruckman

STATEMENT #150. (pp. 204-205) *"As more information becomes known, the 'KJV-only' position must create more explanations that are regularly borrowed from Peter Ruckman in order to maintain their insistence that Blayney's 1769 KJV Revision or Scrivener's 1881 TR revision are perfect."*

COMMENT #150. Sproul is wedding Ruckmanism with my position and others wrongfully and saying erroneously that we both are part of the *"'KJV-only' position*. This is patently false.

I have never ascribed *"perfection"* or *"inspiration"* to the King James Bible as Ruckman and others have done. I do ascribe *"perfection"* to the original, preserved, inerrant, infallible Hebrew, Aramaic, and Greek Words underlying the King James Bible.

Though Sproul does not agree with my position, he is under clear obligation to present it accurately and not to mingle it with the position of Peter Ruckman or some of his followers in the *"KJV-only"* position that he leads.

CHAPTER FIVE: GOD COMMUNICATES THROUGH AN "UNCLEAN THING?" (pp. 207-245)

"Surrett" Not A Strong "TR Proponent"

STATEMENT #151. (pp. 207, 225) This is the beginning of Chapter 5. Its title is: *"God Communicates Through an 'Unclean Thing'?--Questionable Theologians Who Are Key in Formulating 'KJV-only' Theology.... Surrett, a strong KJV and TR proponent asserts..."*

COMMENT #151. Charles Surrett is a teacher at Ambassador Baptist College. I would not consider him a *"strong KJV and TR proponent."* In this quote, Surrett is destroying Psalm 12:6-7 as a proof of Bible preservation. He wrote a book entitled *Which Greek Text?* In that book, he tried to present both sides of the subject with the strongest emphasis in favor of the critical Greek text. This is certainly not a *"strong"* stand. You will not read or hear from my pen or tapes any favorable words for the Westcott and Hort text, the United Bible Societies text, the Nestle/Aland text, or any of the other critical texts of our day.

Ted Letis An Enemy of the DBS

STATEMENT #152. (p. 228) Sproul has a section named: *"Theodore Letis."*

COMMENT #152. Why did Sproul list the late Theodore Letis along with Frederick Nolan, Dr. David Otis Fuller, Dean John Burgon, or Benjamin Wilkinson? Theodore Letis was against our Dean Burgon Society. He was against those of us who are Baptists. He was against Bible separation. He was against me. Theodore Letis was asked by Pensacola Christian College to be on video with Del Johnson to talk on textual matters. They should have never had Theodore Letis. He was a neo-evangelical Lutheran whose denomination was connected with the apostate National and World Councils of Churches. I don't know why Sproul brought Letis into this subject. Though Letis claimed to use the King James Bible when he was in the Pensacola Video, but he also pushed the King James 21st Century Bible. He was the media representative for the KJ21.

CHAPTER SIX:
GOD COMMUNICATES
THROUGH ACCURATE
INFORMATION
(pp. 247-278)

"KJV-only"--Ruckman Smear Term

STATEMENT #153. (pp. 248-249) This begins Chapter 6. The title is: *"God Communicates Through Accurate Information--Three Major Fallacies of the 'KJV-only' Position."* Sproul wrote: *"Many historical and logical fallacies exist in the <u>'KJV-only' arguments.</u>"*

    COMMENT #153. Again, let me repeat, I am not part of the "<u>KJV-only Position</u>" which is linked to its alleged leader, Peter Ruckman. Sproul lists "*three major failings*" in this position.

David Cloud Is Wrong Here

STATEMENT #154. (p. 249) Sproul quoted David Cloud as follows: *"We are convinced that the KJV is accurate in all textual matters, and if there is a difference between the KJV reading and any certain edition of the Received Text, <u>we follow the KJV.</u>"*

    COMMENT #154. On most matters, I agree with David Cloud. However, (if this is an accurate quotation from David Cloud) I would differ with him on this point, as I differ with him on a few other points. Where the Received Text and the King James Bible might differ (and there are very few places, if any, where this might occur), he can follow the King James Bible if he wants to, but I would follow the Words of the Received Text underlying the King James Bible. This taking of the KJB over the Received Text is a dangerous position which is taken by Peter Ruckman and his followers. David Cloud states that he is not one of Ruckman's followers, but I do not think he should side with Ruckman in this area. **It was not the King James Bible that was "*inspired*" or "*God-breathed*" but the Hebrew, Aramaic, and Greek Words underlying**

it that were "*inspired*," "*God-breathed*," and "*given by inspiration of God*." These Greek Words must always be the foundation of any translation in any language, including English.

God Has Preserved His Words

STATEMENT #155. (p. 251) Sproul wrote concerning a quote by Kent Brandenburg, "The 'KJV-only' argument makes these claims: '**If God promises to preserve His Word** and our godly Christian forefathers have always had the KJV/ TR, then God's definition of preservation must be the same as ours. [*i.e., every Word be accessible in every generation*]; *therefore, the KJV and or the TR is inerrant because we use it today. God would never let His church lose a perfect Bible or go astray concerning the Bible.*"

COMMENT #155. Though Sproul and his Fundamentalist doubters deny it, God did promise to "*preserve His Words*." Many Bible verses promise this (Cf. Matthew 24:35; Mark 13:31; and Luke 21:33 and many other verses).

> It is also true that God's Words have always been "*accessible.*" This does not mean that every one in the world had access to them, even as it is true now that His Words are "*accessible*" in English in the King James Bible, even though not everyone has seen these Words. They could if they would. So it was with the Hebrew, Aramaic, and Greek Words underlying the KJB. They were always accessible despite the fact that not all could read them.

Though I say that the Hebrew, Aramaic, and Greek Words underlying the KJB are "*inerrant, infallible, inspired, and preserved,*" I never use these words for anything that man has put his hand upon, including Bible translations--even the accurate King James Bible.

Critical Text--"Fewer" MSS Than TR

STATEMENT #156. (p. 252) "*The older document has passed through fewer human hands, and a case can be made for the fewer older manuscripts being more authentic. The overwhelming majority of mainstream Separatist leaders between A. D. 1875--1980 interpret Scripture in such a way that lead them to prefer the fewer older manuscripts.*"

COMMENT #156. Notice that Sproul admits he has "*fewer older manuscripts.*" As to how much "*fewer,*" let me put it into perspective

> Going back to 1967 (and the percentage would no doubt remain the same today), Kurt Aland had copies of 5,255 Greek manuscripts at Munster Germany. According to the analysis of Dr. Jack Moorman in his book, *Forever Settled* (BFT #1428 for a gift of $20.00), 5,210 (over 99%) of these go along with the Traditional Received Text and only 45 (less than 1%) of these go along with the Critical text of either Westcott and Hort, Nestle/Aland, or

the United Bible Societies.

Then Sproul says that the "_overwhelming majority of mainstream_ _Separatist leaders_" prefer the Vatican ("B") and the Sinai ("Aleph") manuscripts (and about forty-three others) and the false critical texts based upon them. Question: Even if the statement were true (and I question it), does that make it correct? Of course not. The only thing that makes this position correct or incorrect is Truth based on the facts of the case, and certainly not on opinion, even that of "_Fundamentalist leaders._" If they believed as Sproul asserted it, they are wrong. It is as simple as that.

God Has Preserved His WORDS

STATEMENT #157. (p. 253) *"The kind question to ask any of my friends in the 'KJV-only' movement is this: Could your interpretation of Scriptural passages that you use as proof text to discuss God's preservation of His Word be in error? Fundamentalists agree that God preserved His Word, but what verse literally teaches_the method of preservation_ or the _location of the preserved Word_ except 'in Heaven' [Psalm 119:89]."*

COMMENT #157. The question I would ask of Sproul and his Fundamentalist friends would be whether or not their interpretation of these Scriptural passages could be in error? I believe this is the case.

> Notice Sproul referred again only to "_God's preservation of His Word_'" rather than "_His Words._" He used this same term in the title of his book, *God's _Word_ Preserved.* By "_Word_," Sproul and the other Fundamentalist critical text leaders do not mean God's "_Words_" but only God's "*ideas, thoughts, concepts, message, truth, or teachings.*" There is a world of difference between these two things.

Matthew 24:35; Mark 13:31; and Luke 21:33 and many other verses make it crystal clear that "_the method of preservation_" has to do with the Hebrew, Aramaic, and Greek Words rather than mere "*ideas, thoughts, concepts, message, truth, or teachings.*"

> As for the "_location of the preserved Word[s]_," it is so simple that a child can understand it. The "_location of the preserved Word[s]_," is with the more than 99% (5,210 manuscripts) of the "*Words*" which He has "*preserved*" rather than with the less than 1% (45 manuscripts) of the "*Words.*" By any intelligent definition of "*preserved*" less than 1% does not qualify, but more than 99% certainly does.

No "Contortions"--Doctrine Involved

STATEMENT #158. (p. 254) *"All of those contortions of theological and historical integrity are necessary simply for the 'KJV-only' movement to* preserve nearly <u>*two thousand words*</u> that <u>*do not affect one doctrine*</u> that is [sic] clearly explained in another passage of Scripture, and often in numerous passages."

COMMENT #158. Again, I am not part of the "KJV-only movement" that Sproul uses as a smear term. It is he that is guilty of "<u>*contortions of theological and historical integrity*</u>," not I.

Sproul has made a "*contortion*" and a denial of "*historical integrity*" by saying there are merely "<u>*two thousand words*</u>" of differences that are involved between his preferred critical text and the Traditional Words underlying our King James Bible. Though this is not measured in "*words*," **it is a fact that there are over 8,000 differences.** These are tabulated specifically in Dr. Jack Moorman's book, *8,000 Differences Between the Textus Receptus and the Critical Text* (**BFT #3084 @ $20.00 + S&H**).

Sproul has also made a "*contortion*" and a denial of "*historical integrity*" by saying that these differences "<u>*do not affect one doctrine*</u>" not taught elsewhere. In the first place, Sproul is diminishing the number of passages that are doctrinal in content. Secondly, he doesn't think the doctrines should be everywhere they are to be found. I differ strongly on this. The doctrines should never be dropped out or polluted in any way. Dr. Jack Moorman again has found 356 doctrinal passages where Sproul's critical text is in error. This is found in two of Dr. Moorman's books:

1. *356 Doctrinal Errors in the NIV & Other Versions* (**BFT #2956 for a gift of $10.00 + S&H**), and
2. *Early Manuscripts, Church Fathers, and the Authorized Version* (**BFT #3230 for a gift of $20.00**, pages 119-312).

Although I have not researched it exhaustively, among these 356 doctrinal passages, there are some doctrines that are not taught in the same manner elsewhere in the New Testament as Sproul asserts that they are.

I Don't Use "Perfect" For the KJB

STATEMENT #159. (p. 255) Sproul wrote about Pastor Cairns a Free Presbyterian Pastor from Greenville, SC: "*He accurately presents, from a strong KJV position, the reason he does not believe every word of Blayney's 1769 revision is perfect, and by extension every word in Scrivener's TR.*"

COMMENT #159. I do not use the word "*perfect*" in referring to anything that man has made, including the King James Bible. I don't say it is "*imperfect*," but I reserve the "*perfect*" term for God's doings. "*As for God, His way is perfect . . .*" (Psalm 18:30a) **I do use the word, "*perfect*," for the Words underlying the King James Bible**, but I cannot prove it conclusively to those who wish to take another view.

No Translators' "Inspirational Powers"

STATEMENT #160. (p. 255) *"Whether one wishes the KJV's TR's perfection or the __KJV's perfection__ the result is the same: Anglican priests __with inspirational powers__ perfectly selected certain words from the Latin and placed them in English and Greek without any Greek manuscript evidence."*

COMMENT #160. Sproul has told a blatant lie here. No one has *"__inspirational powers__,"* and certainly not the King James Bible translators. How can this chairman of a board of a Baptist college lie this way? I do not believe in the *"__KJV's perfection__"* either. *"Perfection"* for me and others who agree with me lies in the Hebrew, Aramaic, and Greek Words underlying the King James Bible, and not in any translation of those Words. *"Perfection"* lies in those underlying Words and not in the English translation.

Another lie that Sproul states here is that the King James Bible translators took *"certain words"* from Latin and put them in *"English and Greek."* He does not elaborate on this. To some one reading this sentence, it would seem that Sproul was saying that our King James Bible was based on Latin rather than Hebrew, Aramaic, and Greek which is totally untrue. Our Bible is translated from Hebrew, Aramaic, and Greek, not Latin as this sentence seems to imply without further clarification.

Greek Texts Are "Really the Issue"

STATEMENT #165. (p. 256) *"But the Greek text is not the same; Blayney's 1769 Revision is the concern. . . . __Since the Greek text is not really the issue__ except to justify their pre-conceived goal of maintaining __Blayney's 1769 revision of the 1611__, logical, Scriptural, or historical inconsistency is not a problem to the __leaders of the 'KJV-only' movement__."*

COMMENT #165. Again, I am not in any way a part of the so-called *"'__KJV-only' movement__"* which is used as a smear term to be applied by Fundamentalists who are critical text worshipers to many of us who are not Ruckmanites in order to condemn us.

> Sproul is totally false when he wrote: *"__Since the Greek text is not really the issue__ . . . ."* Though for the Ruckmanites this is true, for me and others who stand for the King James Bible and the Greek Words underlying it, the Greek text most certainly is *"__the issue__."* This is why the critical text has been refuted repeatedly in my books and other authors' books as well.

I, and others who agree, hold *"__Blayney's 1769 revision of the 1611__"* as the only accurate translation of the Hebrew, Aramaic, and Greek Words that underlie it. But we do not say it *"corrects"* the original languages, nor do we say it is a special and *"advanced revelation"* as Ruckman and his followers teach. This is Ruckmanite heresy. In order to have a good translation in any language, you must start with accurate textual words. That is what we have in our King James Bible. The KJB translators began with accurate Words of Hebrew, Aramaic, and Greek.

Perfect God and Perfect Man

STATEMENT #166. (p. 258, footnote 23) Sproul, explaining the *"hypostatic union"* of the Lord Jesus Christ, wrote: *"This means Jesus existed in human form as 100% God and 100% man."*

COMMENT #166. What Sproul should have said was that in the *"hypostatic union"* the Lord Jesus Christ combined two natures in one Person. He had a perfect Human nature and a perfect Divine nature. He was perfect Man and also perfect God. He had perfect Humanity and perfect Deity. I believe that is more accurate than using the "100%" terms which really means a totality. Technically, you cannot have two 100%'s in one whole, but two wholes.

No Translator "Inspirational Powers"

STATEMENT #167. (p. 259) *"Not even those <u>translators</u> whose <u>products, vested with 'inspirational powers' by KJV-onlyism</u>, believed Christians should have such 'faith' about their work."*

COMMENT #167. This idea about the KJB <u>translators'</u> products being "<u>vested with 'inspirational powers' by KJV-onlyism</u>" is pure Ruckmanism which I and many others of us deny. God did not *"breathe out"* or *"inspire"* the King James Bible. He only *"breathed out"* or *"inspired"* the original Hebrew, Aramaic, and Greek.

DBS Not "Opposed" To Dean Burgon

STATEMENT #168. (p. 260) Sproul wrote about Ted Letis again: *"Letis . . . exposes the Dean Burgon Society as <u>being opposed to its own namesake</u>."*

COMMENT #168. Dr. David Otis Fuller, Pastor E. L. Bynum, and I organized the Dean Burgon Society (DBS) in 1978. I have been the President of the DBS from the beginning. It is entirely false to paint the DBS as "<u>being opposed to its own namesake</u>, Dean John W. Burgon. We are not named the Dean Burgon Society because of anything else but his opposition to the false Westcott and Hort Greek text, to the English Revised Version, and his support of the Traditional Greek text and the Authorized Version.

The DBS has brought back into print five of Dean Burgon's books in hardback format. That does not indicate that we are *"opposed"* to him. If either Sproul or the late Ted Letis can come up with documented proof of this charge, I would be glad to see it. There is no proof of it because it is false.

At the bottom of the page of every issue of our *Dean Burgon News*, we print the following words: *"THE DEAN BURGON SOCIETY, INC., proudly takes its name in honor of John William Burgon 1813-1888, the Dean of Chichester in England, whose tireless and accurate scholarship and contribution in the area of New Testament Textual Criticism; whose defense of the Traditional Greek New Testament Text against the many enemies; and whose firm belief in the verbal inspiration and inerrancy of the Bible; we believe, have all been unsurpassed either before or since his time."*

"Majority Text" Not Burgon's

STATEMENT #169. (p. 262) Sproul quoted Ted Letis once again: *"I have collated this revised edition of the T.R. produced by Burgon and Miller with another revision that appeared back in 1982, the Majority Text, which was an attempt to further the work that Burgon had begun."*

COMMENT #169. This is absolutely false and misleading. There is no such thing as a "*T.R. produced by Burgon and Miller.*" Letis is referring to a small booklet, which the Bible For Today has reproduced. It is by Edward Miller, and not by Dean Burgon. Miller had some suggested changes in the book of Matthew that he published after the death of Dean Burgon and therefore, without Burgon's approval. Burgon's method was extensive and he said it could not be done right even during his lifetime for various reasons. He was content to leave the Textus Receptus as it stands.

As for "*the Majority Text*" furthering "*the work that Burgon had begun,*" this is entirely false because Hodges and Farstad refused to abide by Dean Burgon's specific principles in that work in 1982. **For a specific list of how Dean Burgon would have gone about any revision of the Textus Receptus, you can find it in BFT #804,** *Burgon's Warnings on Revision* **for a gift of $7.00 + $4.00 S&H.** They did not do it correctly in many ways. They did not examine all of the uncials. They did not examine all of the cursives or even a good portion of them. They did not examine all of the papyri. They did not examine all of the quotations from the early church fathers. They neglected many other cautions that Dean Burgon set forth clearly.

Do you know how many manuscripts Hodges and Farstad consulted? They did not look at any manuscripts themselves. Do you know what they did? They took as gospel the work of one man named Hermann Von Soden, a German apostate unbeliever. Von Soden was slipshod and inaccurate in his work as even his friends agreed. Hodges and Farstad relied heavily on Von Soden's notes for their approximately 1,800 differences from the Textus Receptus. Von Soden used only 414 manuscripts out of 5,255 that were available as of 1967. 414 is by no means a "*majority*" of 5,255. So why is it called "*The Majority Text*"? For an excellent analysis of the failures of this "**Majority Text**," you should get **BFT #1617**, *Hodges and Farstad's Majority Text Refuted* by Dr. Jack Moorman for a gift of $16.00 + $5.00 S&H.

The "Septuagint" Was A.D., Not B.C.

STATEMENT #170. (p. 264) Sproul has a heading that reads: "*Did Jesus, the Apostles, and the Early Christians Have the Bible?*" Referring to Psalm 8:2 and Matthew 21:16, Sproul then says: "*These verses are not identical. It seems Jesus is quoting from a different translation! Jesus' Old Testament quotation clearly comes from the Septuagint.*"

COMMENT #170. I believe Sproul is clearly in error when he stated that "*Jesus' Old Testament quotation clearly comes from the Septuagint.*" The Septuagint was not in existence when the Lord Jesus Christ was on this earth. How could He quote from something that did not exist? There may have been a few books of the Hebrew Bible that had been translated into the Greek, but not the whole 39 Old Testament books. They cannot prove that the whole Septuagint from Genesis through Malachi existed in the time of Christ. The only complete translation of the Hebrew Old Testament into Greek was in A.D., not B.C. It is in the 5th column of the 6th columns of Origin's Hexapla. The Lord Jesus Christ did not quote from it. If anything, the Hexapla quoted from Jesus and the Apostles.

Perfect TR Is Scrivener's TR

STATEMENT #171. (p. 265) One of Sproul's captions reads: "*Where is this 'perfect' or 'exact' Received Text located and what or who determines the identification of this text?*" Sproul then said: "*If preservation is perfection in one place, then where is the preserved 'KJV-only' Bible? If it is located in the 1611 KJV, which revision? If it is in the TR, which printer or revision of the TR has it?*"

COMMENT #171. In answer to the question, "*Where is this 'perfect' or 'exact' Received Text located,*" I have identified it in my belief as the Hebrew, Aramaic, and Greek Words underlying the King James Bible. This Greek text is basically Beza's 5th edition of 1598. It is the text published by Dr. Frederick Scrivener and republished by the Dean Burgon Society. It is called *Scrivener's Annotated Greek New Testament* (#1670 @ $35.00 + $5.00 S&H). I define my terms when I say the Traditional Text or the Byzantine Text or the Textus Receptus Text is the text, which underlies our King James Bible.

I have been investigating this subject since 1970. After reading and studying widely, I have come to believe and to hold as my personal conviction that those Greek Words mentioned above for the New Testament are the original and preserved Words of the New Testament writers. The Lord Jesus Christ promised to preserve His Old and New Testament Words (Matthew 24:35; Mark 13:31; Luke 21:33 and other places). I believe it is incumbent upon us to seek to find those preserved Words. I have found them to my own satisfaction in the Words underlying the King James Bible. I believe the facts in the case point to this text, but I cannot convince others to adopt it if they choose other Words or have no Words at all on which they can depend.

"Heretic" Is Not Just "Schismatic"

STATEMENT #172. (p. 265) *"Having the 'right' genealogical transmission line is so important to those of the 'KJV-only' position. Right after the command to 'avoid foolish questions and genealogies' is verse ten. 'A man that is an heretic after the first and second admonition reject'* [*3:10.*] *The word translated 'heretic' carries with it the idea of schismatic."*

COMMENT #172. It is extremely false to declare, as Sproul did here that *"in the word translated 'heretic' carries with it the idea of schismatic."* "**Heretic**" is not at all the same as "*schismatic*." The word, "*heretic*" comes from the Greek word HAIREO meaning "*to hold*." It means to hold a doctrine or doctrines that are false. That's what a heretic is.

> **Sproul is saying that those of us who stand for our King James Bible and the Hebrew, Aramaic, and Greek Words underlying it are "*heretics*" and "*schismatics*" both. Both charges are false.**

In 2001 there was a resolution at the Fundamental Baptist Fellowship (FBF), with which Sproul is an officer, that implied the same false conclusion. In that resolution, they talked about the *"brethren"* in quotation marks, implying that the Fundamentalists who stand for the King James Bible and its underlying Words are "*heretics*" and "*schismatics*." The resolution was calling Fundamental Bible-believing brethren "*heretics*" who should be "*rejected.*"

STATEMENT #173. (p. 266) *"One who strives and divides churches about matters that fall into the category of Deuteronomy 29:29 might be categorized under the heading of 'heretic.'"*

COMMENT #173. Deuteronomy 29:29 is a good verse. It says:

> *"The secret things belong unto the LORD our God: but those things which are revealed belong unto us and to our children for ever, that we may do all the words of this law."*

This verse is a wish by the Jews "*that we may do all the words of this law.*" It is a verse for the preservation of "*all the Words of this law.*" This a verse that speaks of the need for verbal, plenary preservation of God's Words which I believe and Sproul denies. I see no application in this verse to "*heretics.*"

"One who strives and divides churches" cannot rightly be called a "*heretic.*" As I have stated before, a "*heretic*" is one who hold doctrines that are unbiblical. Sproul has a phony idea as to what a heretic is. He thinks that if a person does not agree with him that person is a heretic. This is a false teaching.

"TR Readings" Are Not "Minority"

STATEMENT #174. (p. 271) Sproul has a heading entitled: "*'KJV-only' theory #1.*" Under this heading he wrote: "*. . . therefore, minority TR readings take precedence over literally hundreds of manuscripts.*" Footnote #57 reads: "*This appears to be a theory adopted by Waite, Sorenson, Surrett, and Brandenburg.*"

COMMENT #174. Notice that Sproul erroneously and purposely links me with this "*'KJV-only' Theory #1.*" This *"KJV-only"* is a smear term for Ruckmanites which certainly does not represent my views.

The Textus Receptus manuscripts do not reflect "*minority TR readings.*" Quite the contrary. Of the 5,255 manuscripts cataloged in 1967 by Kurt Aland, Dr. Jack Moorman, in his book, *Forever Settled*, shows that over 99% (5,210) of these go along with the Received Words underlying the King James Bible. That is far from a "*minority TR readings.*"

Sproul's Critical Greek text has less than 1% (45) of these manuscripts to back up his false readings. Which one is really the "*minority*"? Here, as in other places, Sproul is giving the opposite of the truth, which by definition is a lie.

We Can Stand Exegetical "Scrutiny"

STATEMENT #175. (p. 272) Sproul wrote: "*. . . even if the 'KJV-only' position cannot stand the scrutiny of biblical exegesis, history, or logic, a Christian is obliged to believe it based only on faith.*" Sproul has a footnote #58 which reads: "*This is the position of Khoo, Waite, Cloud, and Brandenburg.*"

COMMENT #175. Again Sproul is wrongly identifying me with the "*'KJV-only' position.*" My own position certainly can indeed "*stand the scrutiny of biblical exegesis, history, and logic.*"

No Placement of "English" to "Greek"

STATEMENT #176. (p. 273) "*No verse states that God will 'providentially guide' Anglican Priests (or anyone) to the 'exact' words of Scripture in its entirety, some without any Greek or Hebrew authentication, and then additionally lead F. H. A. Scrivener to perfectly place these English words back into Greek some three hundred years later so the world would have for the first time in one place a perfect Greek representative of the autographs.*"

COMMENT #176. One of the most arrogant statements Sproul has repeated repeatedly in his book is the charge that something "*lead F. H. A. Scrivener to perfectly place these English words back into Greek some three hundred years later.*" He has not a shred of proof that Scrivener put any "*English words back into Greek.*" As I have pointed out repeatedly, Dr.

Frederick Scrivener's Greek text is based upon the 5th edition of Beza dated in 1598. He did not do any English to Greek translation. In only 190 places recorded in the Appendix (out of over 140,000 words) was some other source used.

KJB Translators Were Not the "Authors"

STATEMENT #177. (p. 274) "... *it is not Biblical to assert for Scrivener or the 1611 translators the guidance that only the original authors of Scripture claim.*"

COMMENT #177. Sproul is in serious error to call the human writers "*the original authors of Scripture*." He should have written "*original WRITERS of Scripture*." They were not "*authors.*" The Lord Jesus Christ was the "*Author.*"

According to John 16:12-14, the Author of the entire New Testament was the Lord Jesus Christ Himself. By extension, He, as the Logos and Revelator, was also the Author of the Old Testament. He gave the Words to the Holy Spirit and the Holy Spirit then gave the Words to the human writers such as Matthew, Mark, Luke, John, Paul, Jude, and Peter.

No Claim For "Inerrant Guidance"

STATEMENT #178. (p. 274) "*Believing in 'inerrant guidance' for the KJV translators in their Greek or English choices is without historical precedence among Separatists.*"

COMMENT #178. Sproul is falsely accusing people like me of believing in "*'inerrant guidance' for the KJV translators in their Greek or English choices*." No human being, whether the "*KJV translators*" or any others can rightly claim "*inerrant guidance*." This charge by Sproul aimed at me and others who stand with me is ridiculous. He does not have one bit of evidence to support that I believe this.

Waite/Ruckman Link Is A Smear

STATEMENT #179. (p. 274) Sproul quoted Brandenburg when he wrote: "'*In the oracles of men only glorify men.' Brandenburg must make statements like this to attack those who site the Fundamentalist and Separatist Fathers because his interpretation is unknown to Baptists and separatists until less than fifty years ago. Brandenburg, Waite, Cloud, Sorenson, Grady, Riplinger, Ruckman and others have set themselves up as the authorities to overthrow four hundred years of Baptist Separatists thought on the subject of inerrancy and preservation.*"

COMMENT #179. Sproul continues to glorify human beings such as "*Fundamentalist and Separatist Fathers*" rather than the Words of God in the Bible.

Notice how Sproul puts "*Waite*" in the same breath with "*Ruckman*." This is what he has been doing throughout the book. He has been putting me (and every other person who has a similar sound position on the King James Bible and its underlying Hebrew, Aramaic, and Greek Words) into the "*KJV-only*" Ruckman bag and discards us. I am strongly opposed to Peter Ruckman's position, and he is opposed to mine. How can Sproul dare to put me and others in the same sentence?!

Sproul's book title is "*God's Word Preserved*." How can he berate some of us who believe God has both promised and fulfilled His promise of the preservation of his original Hebrew, Aramaic, and Greek Words? How can he use the word "*Preserved*" in his title when he denies that the Bible has been "*Preserved*"? When will his hypocrisy end?

Sproul's False "Preservation"

STATEMENT #180. (p. 276) "*T
he second fallacy involves the definition of preservation; that preservation extended to a perfectly preserved text, and or version in our hands today.*"

COMMENT #180. Even though Sproul does not agree with the definition of "*preservation,*" this is exactly what "*preservation*" means. Sproul is fooling his readers by the very title of his book, *God's Word Preserved*. What he really means is that "*God's Word*" (in the clear sense of His **Words**) has not been "*preserved*." He just means that God's "*ideas, thoughts, concepts, message, truth, or teachings,*" have been "*preserved*," but not His **Words**. That, my dear reader, is not "*preservation*" at all! It is a deceptive, false, and lying title. I believe God promised to "*preserve*" a *perfectly preserved text*, including all the Hebrew, Aramaic, and Greek Words. My definition of the Word of God is the Hebrew, Aramaic and Greek Words of God. The Lord Jesus promised: "*Heaven and earth shall pass away, but my Words shall not pass away*" (Matthew 24:35; Mark 13:31; Luke 21:33; Matthew 5:18-19). My Saviour does not lie. He meant what He said (in all three of these exactly the same verses), and He said what He meant. He has promised a "*perfectly preserved text*."

It is Scrivener's TR

STATEMENT #181. (p. 276) "*Which revision of the TR or KJV has it? [If the TR], 'which TR?'*"

COMMENT #181. I have pointed out repeatedly that I believe the preserved Hebrew, Aramaic, and Greek Words are those underlying the King James Bible. It is really quite simple. With the exception of about 190 places, the New Testament Greek Words are found in Beza's 5th edition Greek text of 1598.

"KJV-only" = Ruckmanism

STATEMENT #182. (p. 276) *"Without the 'Waldensian theory' of history . . . the minority reading* **the 'KJV-only' theology** *must sink into Ruckman's double inspiration as a rationale for its attacks on both the older Alexandrian minority reading and the younger Byzantine majority readings."*

COMMENT #182. Again Sproul brings up "**the 'KJV-only' theology**" as being yoked up with "***Ruckman's double inspiration***." And once again, I renounce the smear term, "***the 'KJV-only' theology***," as well as "***Ruckman's double inspiration***."

> If Sproul wants to battle with Peter Ruckman and his heretical views, he should single him out and write a book against him. If Sproul wants to battle with me and others like me who have a contrary position on the Bible and Bible Preservation, and yet oppose Ruckman and Ruckmanites, he should write a book against us. But to put both groups into his present book and imply that we are one is the height of "*bearing false witness*" and falsehood.

I have a completely contrary position on Bibliology from Sproul and from Ruckman. I refute "***double inspiration***." God's "*breathing out*" or "*inspiring*" His Hebrew, Aramaic, and Greek Words occurred only once. It did not occur in the translation of the King James Bible or in any other translation. The translators of the King James Bible took those God-breathed and preserved Hebrew, Aramaic, and Greek Words and translated them accurately.

Words Under the KJB=Original Text

STATEMENT #183. (p. 277) Speaking of the "*KJV-only*" camp, Sproul wrote: *". . . but they do accept the 1611 translators' Greek and Hebrew choices as identical to the original text of Scripture."*

COMMENT #183. What's wrong with that? I would certainly agree with that. As I have said before, my belief is that the exact "**preservation**" of the original Hebrew, Aramaic, and Greek Words is anchored on those Words underlying the King James Bible.

> Where does Sproul anchor his "preservation"? He has written an entire book on "*God's Word Preserved*" and yet he has never told us where it is "*preserved*." Sproul has no anchor. He is adrift. He doesn't know where God's Words are or where they are not, and yet he blasts away at those of us who do have an anchor and a firm foundation amidst the stormy waves of unbelief today.

In this regard, he is very little different from the worst apostates and unbelievers who have ever lived. They have no Bible anchor either.

"Anglican Priests" Not "Perfect"

STATEMENT #184. (p. 277) *"Ruckman accepts the perfection of the* ***Anglican priest's*** [sic] *choices in English, and the 'KJV-only' advocates believe* ***these same priests***, *who persecuted godly Separatists, had perfect insight in Greek and Hebrew choices. Both views accept* ***perfection*** *of Anglican priests."*

COMMENT #184. Apparently, Sproul has great hatred against the King James Bible translators. He calls them "***Anglican priests***." I am not sure they were all "***priests***" of the Church of England at that time. I do not believe the"***perfection***" of any person living or dead (including Sproul) except the Lord Jesus Christ. Regardless of the church affiliation of the King James Bible translators, I as an independent and Fundamental Baptist Pastor, have confidence in their collective linguistic abilities which far exceed those of Sproul or any other living person in the world today. They were certainly superior. Sproul need not drag the rabbit trail of alleged "***persecution of godly Separatists***" by "***these same priests***." In the first place, Sproul alleges no proof of his serious charge, which has no foundation in fact. The second place, even if true (which it is not), this would have nothing to do with their translation work during 1604 through 1611 and should not be introduced into this subject. I do stand for the Hebrew, Aramaic, and Greek Words that underlie our King James Bible, and I believe the King James Bible is the only accurate translation of those Words.

CHAPTER SEVEN: GOD COMMUNICATES BY KEEPING HIS WORD SAFE (pp. 279-327)

Sproul Uses "Word," Not "Words"

STATEMENT #185. (pp. 279-281) Chapter 7, "*God Communicates by Keeping His Word Safe--God's Providential Care of His Word.*" On page 281, Sproul asked a series of questions: "*What are the meanings of words that surround the theology of preservation? Did God preserve His Word for modern Christians? How did He accomplish this preservation? Can Christians rest assured that God has kept His Word so that believers today can obey all that He wishes them to do with joy? Can a Christian depend on God to keep His promises? Where will one find God's preserved Word?*"

COMMENT #185. Notice that Sproul refers three times in this quote to "*His Word*" and once to "*God's preserved Word*." I am certain that most of Sproul's readers will think that he means "*His Words*" and "*God's preserved Words,*" but he does not. He refers only to God's "*ideas, thoughts, concepts, message, truth, or teachings,*" but not "*His Words.*" This is major deception on Sproul's part because, to this point in his book, he has never come clean and told his readers his unique and untenable definition of "*God's Word*" or "*God's preserved Word.*" He is playing word games without even so much as a hint of warning to his readers. Without a clear definition of terms from the very outset of his book, the very title of his book, *God's Word Preserved*, is a serious and gross deception that has been perpetrated on his unsuspecting readers who are not looking for clever semantic prevarication.

More Than Words From "Destruction"

STATEMENT #186. (p. 283) The title of this section is: "*Preservation.*" Sproul's first sentence in this section is: "*Preservation is God's protection of all His Words from destruction through geographic distribution, independent witnesses, and a multiplicity of copies.*"

COMMENT #186. For a change, Sproul is speaking of God's "*Words*" rather than just His "*Word.*" He is concerned here, not with "*perfection*" of these "*Words*" but only the "*protection of all His Words from destruction.*" Sproul does not know where these "*Words*" are today and he doesn't want me or anyone else to know where they are either. But I **do** know where They are, and Sproul despises me because of it.

Original Words Must Be the Base

STATEMENT #187. (p. 283) "*Accurate and faithful copies of God's Word have appeared in many languages through the ages, but they do not agree with one another word for word. The Greek New Testament or the Hebrew Old Testament often formed the basis of a new language version, but often another language other than Greek or Hebrew became the donor language. For example the Septuagint.*"

COMMENT #187. Sproul shows clearly what he means by "*God's Word*" when he stated: "*Accurate and faithful copies of God's Word have appeared in many languages through the ages.*" The only languages that have "*God's Words*" are Hebrew, Aramaic, and Greek. Other languages would be **translations** of God's Words. In this sentence Sproul is reaffirming that he means by "*Word*" of God, only the "*ideas, thoughts, concepts, message, truth, or teachings*" which can appear in other languages. I differ with Sproul also on the date of the Septuagint. He believes it originated in B.C., and I in A.D. in the 5th column of Origen's *Hexapla*.

"Some Men" Did "Delete" Doctrines

STATEMENT #188. (p. 284) "*Some critics claim that at certain times in history, specifically in Egypt in the second and third centuries, some men tried to remove words in order to delete different doctrines from the Bible.*"

COMMENT #188. That is exactly what was done by the Gnostics of Egypt. Any doctrine not believed by their heretical framework was either deleted in the manuscripts they had or the manuscripts were changed to conform to their doctrine. This explains why the Vatican and Sinai Manuscripts have over 356 doctrinal passages where doctrine is altered in some large or small way. It is good that these Gnostics of Alexandria, Egypt did not have all of the New Testament manuscripts with which to conform to their errors. As a result of the Gnostic tampering (as attested by many early Church Fathers) the Critical Text represented by the Vatican and the Sinai manuscripts have dropped out no less than 2,886 Greek Words.

Heretic Corruption Is Documented

STATEMENT #189. (p. 285) After Sproul talks about the heretic, Marcion, who "*attempted to delete parts*" of the Bible, he wrote: ". . . *no primary source exists that indicates that heretics attempted to remove certain words relating to individual doctrines in Egypt or any manuscripts that Christians have today.*"

> **COMMENT #189.** Dean John W. Burgon wrote an entire book entitled *the Causes of Corruption of the Traditional Text*. In this book, Dean Burgon outlines five causes of "*accidental corruption*" and ten causes of "*intentional corruption.*" This is certainly a "*primary source*" of evidence on this problem.

It can be obtained as #1160 @ $16.00 + $5.00 S&H. You can call 1-800-John 10:9 with your credit card and get a copy. One of the causes of corruption was because of heretics. When they changed the Bible's Words, they made the Words conform to their heresies.

> Dean Burgon mentions over twelve different heretics that have changed and altered the Scripture. It is a matter of historical fact. Sproul is in error in this matter.

False Doctrines Do "Stick Out"

STATEMENT #190. (p. 286) ". . . *however, even if the heretics had attempted to remove some specific doctrines, those changes would 'stick out' like a 'sore thumb' when textual critics collated the vast numbers of manuscripts and their geographic distribution.*"

COMMENT #190. Sproul is wrong on this point also when he doesn't think there were "*some specific doctrines*" that are in the Vatican and Sinai Manuscripts and shine forth in the modern versions. Some of them certainly do "*stick out like a sore thumb.*"

> Notice in Philippians 4:13 the removal of the Name of "*Christ*" Who is the only One Who can "*strengthen*" the Christian:
>
> *I can do all things through Christ which strengtheneth me.* (KJV)
> *I can do everything through him who gives me strength.* (NIV)

> Notice in Romans 1:16 the removal once again of the Name of "*Christ*" Whose is the only "*gospel.*"
>
> "*For I am not ashamed of the gospel of Christ: for it is the power of God unto salvation to every one that believeth; to the Jew first, and also to the Greek.*" (KJV)
>
> "*I am not ashamed of the gospel, because it is the power of God for the*

salvation of everyone who believes: first for the Jew, then for the Gentile." (NIV)

Notice in 2 Corinthians 4:14 where there is a serious doctrinal error by changing "*by Jesus*" to "*with Jesus.*"

"*Knowing that he which raised up the Lord Jesus shall raise up us also by Jesus, and shall present us with you.*" (KJV)

"*because we know that the one who raised the Lord Jesus from the dead will also raise us with Jesus and present us with you in his presence.*" (NIV)

The Textus Receptus and the King James Bible proclaim that the saints will be raised "*by Jesus*" as the great Creator. The Critical Text and the New International Version do not portray Christ as the One Who raises the believers. Secondly, if the saints will be raised "*with Jesus*," that would imply that Jesus had not yet been raised and would still be in the grave.

Notice in John 3:15 that the phrase "*should not perish*" is removed by the Critical Text, thus denying a burning perishing Hell for those rejecting Christ.

"*That whosoever believeth in him should not perish, but have eternal life.*" (KJV)

"*that everyone who believes in him [   ] may have eternal life.*" (NIV)

"Alexandrian" Texts Pervert Doctrines

STATEMENT #191. (p. 286) "*Even the 'hated' Alexandrian text type maintains every doctrine. In other words those alleged 'sinister' Alexandrians led by Origin, were not too intelligent because they included the Deity of Christ, for example, in many places.*"

COMMENT #191. In the first place, Sproul says falsely that "*the 'hated' Alexandrian text type maintains every doctrine.* I am not going to list the **356 doctrinal passages** which the "*Alexandrian text type*" (represented by the Vatican and Sinai manuscripts) contains such as in the NIV, NASV, ESV, RSV, NRSV and other modern versions. If you want to see almost **200 pages** listing these **356 doctrinal passages**, get *Early Manuscripts, Church Fathers, and the Authorized Version* (BFT #3230 @ $20.00 + $7.00 S&H) by Dr. Jack Moorman. Turn to **pages 119 to 312** of this 456-page hardback book for these passages.

It is not that the Alexandrian heretic Gnostics were "*not too intelligent.*" The fact is they did not have all the manuscripts and copies of the New Testament in their hands. If they had all of them, they could have changed all of them, but they only had some of the manuscripts and copies. Praise God for that.

The right manuscripts have survived. The churches decided that those Gnostic manuscripts of Egypt that survived for 600 years, were false. This explains why they were not copied and re-copied. Because of this, these "*Alexandrian text type*" of manuscripts form less than 1% of the total. The Textus Receptus manuscripts total over 99% of the current evidence.

"Heretical Intentions" Are Clear

STATEMENT #192. (pp. 286-287) "*If people are to believe the 'KJV-only' position that the Alexandrians had 'sinister' and 'heretical' intentions, then they must also believe that the 'heretical leaders' did not recruit the brightest 'heretics' to do the copying because these 'heretics' left Christ's Deity on their manuscripts many times. They did not remove it from John 1:1 or Titus 2:11-15 and many other clear passages on the Lord's divinity which appear in every text-type.*"

COMMENT #192. From the Gnostic Alexandrian Egyptian manuscripts (Vatican and Sinai), you can clearly see that "*the Alexandrians had 'sinister' and 'heretical' intentions.*" It was these two manuscripts and their followers that placed **356 false doctrinal passages** into the New Testament Greek text. These false doctrinal passages can be seen in the NIV, NASV, ESV, RSV, NRSV, and many other modern versions.

First of all, has Sproul checked on all 356 of these passages? Obviously not. If he has, or if he has not, how does he explain these false doctrines placed in these Gnostic Alexandrian texts? Sproul can buy Dr. Jack Moorman's *Early Manuscripts, Church Fathers, and the Authorized Version* (BFT #3230 @ $20.00 + $7.00 S&H) and look at pages 119-312 for these 356 doctrinal passages with the manuscript authority supporting the readings for the Textus Receptus and those supporting the Critical Text. If Sproul cannot afford Dr. Moorman's book, perhaps he can afford mine. I recommend that he get my *Defending the King James Bible* (BFT #1594 @ $12.00 + $5.00 S&H) and look at Chapter V (pages 131-183) for **158** of the more important of these **356** doctrinal passages.

As for the deity of Christ, the above-listed perversions, following the Vatican and/or the Sinai false manuscripts have most of the following errors and many others regarding the Person and Work of the Lord Jesus Christ:

(1) In 1 Corinthians 15:47, they deny that the Lord Jesus Christ is the "*Lord from Heaven.*"

(2) In 1 Timothy 3:16, they deny that the Lord Jesus Christ is "*God manifest in the flesh.*"

(3) In 1 John 4:3, they deny that the Lord Jesus was "*Christ . . . come*

in the flesh."

(4)   In Matthew 1:25, they deny that the Lord Jesus Christ was the *"First-born Son"* of Mary thus questioning His miraculous virgin birth.

(5)   In Matthew 18:11, in removing the entire verse, they deny that *"the Son of man is come to save that which was lost."*

(6)   In Luke 9:56, in removing the first part of the verse, they remove the truth that the Lord Jesus Christ as the *"Son of man"* did *"not come to destroy men's lives, but to save them."*

(7)   In Luke 2:22, by changing *"her"* purification to *"their"* purification, they imply that the Lord Jesus Christ was a sinner Who needed to be *"purified."*

(8)   In John 7:8, by omitting *"yet"* in the phrase *"I go not up yet,"* and make it read, *"I go not up,"* they, in effect, call the Lord Jesus Christ a liar because in two verse later, He did go up to the feast.

(9)   In Ephesians 3:9, by omitting the words, *"by Jesus Christ"* at the end of that verse, they deny that the Lord Jesus Christ is the Creator of *"all things."*

(10) In John 8:59, by omitting the words *"going through the midst of them, and so passed by,"* they deny that the Lord Jesus Christ was omnipotent and able to pass through a multitude who were trying to kill Him.

(11) In 2 Corinthians 4:14, by changing the word *"by"* Jesus to *"with"* Jesus, they deny that the Lord Jesus Christ was able to raise people from the dead. They also deny that the Lord Jesus Christ was bodily raised from the dead because they say that the Christians will be raised *"with"* Jesus Who is evidently not yet *"raised."*

(12) In Colossians 1:14, by omitting *"through His blood,"* they deny that the Lord Jesus Christ gives believing sinners *"redemption through His blood."*

(13) In 1 Corinthians 5:7, by omitting *"for us"* at the end of the verse, they remove the purpose of the Lord Jesus Christ's being our *"Passover"* and thus deny the His vicarious, substitutionary, expiatory atonement for all the sinners of the world.

(14) In Hebrews 1:3, by omitting *"by Himself,"* they deny that the Lord Jesus Christ alone *"purged our sins"* without the aid of the church, church membership, the saints, the Pope, the pastor, the rabbi, good works, penance, the last rites, Mary, or any of the Roman Catholic saints.

(15) In John 6:47, by omitting "*on Me*," they deny that the Lord Jesus Christ is the only Object of saving faith that brings everlasting life.

The above-fifteen doctrinal problems are only the tip of the iceberg, as they say, with the **356 doctrinal passages** involved in the evidence showing heretical tampering with the original Words of God. It is strange how Sproul is willingly ignorant of the facts in the case in his desire to sugarcoat the Critical Text and those who originated it.

Origen Originated the Septuagint

STATEMENT #193. (p. 288) *"In fact in the incredible Hexapla, 'wicked' Origen wrote the Hebrew side by side with four current Septuagint translations and a Greek transliteration of the Hebrew letters."*

COMMENT #193. Origen's *Hexapla* is the origin of the Septuagint. Origen's approximate dates are about 158-254 A.D. Though it is admitted that a few B.C. writings from Hebrew to Greek have been found, the entire Old Testament B.C. translation from Hebrew to Greek has never been found. The reason for this is that it never happened.

"Origen" Was A Leading Heretic

STATEMENT #194. (p. 288) *"Origen asserts that he spent fifteen years creating the Hexapla to equip Christians in debates with Jews and to protect early believers against the charge they were changing or falsifying the Bible. Origen did not spend his life trying to delete words or phrases but rather invested monumental amounts of time to create an accurate Septuagint for the purpose of evangelizing unbelieving Jews."*

COMMENT #194. It is indeed strange to see Baptist Fundamentalist Sproul defending Gnostic heretic Origen as not tampering with the Words of God to suit his own apostate beliefs. I don't know where Sproul has studied his church history. Origen was one of the most blatant heretics in the Christian Church.

If these early church fathers denied the Scriptures and did not believe in the Received Traditional Text, they did spend their time removing and changing words. That's why there are 2,886 Greek Words less in the Gnostic Alexandrian Critical Text than the Textus Receptus. That's why there are **356 doctrinal passages** involved in their Text compared with the Textus Receptus. That is at least a reason for at least some of the 8,000 differences between the Westcott and Hort Greek Text/Critical Text and the Textus Receptus Greek Text. What Sproul should do to get a grasp on the truth of heretical corruption of the original New Testament Greek Words is to get a copy of Dean John W. Burgon's book, *the*

Causes of Corruption of the Traditional Text (BFT #1160 @ $16.00 + $5.00 S&H). He should read closely Chapter XIII, "*Causes of Corruption Chiefly Intentional IX--Corruption by Heretics*," pages 191-210.

Only Preservation of "Message"?

STATEMENT #195. (pp. 292-293) *"Within fifty years of the original writings, finding every copy and changing the Text became impossible. In the multiplicity of copies, <u>God preserved His Word</u> from the invasions of Muslims, Papist Inquisitions, and sleepy scribes."*

COMMENT #195. Sproul believes that "<u>*God preserved His Word*</u>," but I believe "<u>**God preserved His Hebrew, Aramaic, and Greek Words**</u>." For him, the "<u>*Word*</u>" means only the "*ideas, thoughts, concepts, message, truth, or teachings*," but not the "<u>*Words*</u>." Those original preserved "<u>**Words**</u>" are those underlying our King James Bible rather than the Westcott and Hort's Critical Text or the so-called "*Majority Text*."

STATEMENT #196. (p. 293) The title of this section is: *"How and Where Did God Preserve His Word?"* Sproul says: *"Therefore, <u>God has preserved His Word</u>; it is provable. This probable method of definition of preservation is the fanciful unsubstantiated view of history. The overwhelming evidence to the ancient Text of Scripture dwarfs any other ancient book."*

COMMENT #196. Once again, Sproul only believes that "<u>*God has preserved His Word*</u>," as mentioned in the previous **COMMENT #194**, but not His "<u>Words</u>."

Beware of "Textual Criticism"

STATEMENT #197. (p. 295) *"<u>Textual criticism is the method God choose to preserve His Word</u>. All Bible scholars practice textual criticism today, just as Erasmus and the KJV translators also employed it hundreds of years ago. Comparing and collating manuscripts on doubtful readings is the <u>historic method of preserving God's Word</u> as practiced and <u>taught by the Separatist Fathers</u>."*

COMMENT #197. Sproul is in total error by saying that "<u>*Textual criticism is the method God choose to preserve His Word.*</u>" On the contrary, "<u>*textual criticism*</u>" (as it is now practiced) is man's method of doubting and thus destroying the <u>Words</u> that God has already preserved. God preserved His Words before there was anything called "<u>*textual criticism*</u>." He preserved it in four kinds of Greek manuscripts: (1) uncials (capital letter MSS); (2) cursives (small letter MSS); and (3) lectionaries (MSS read in churches during special church days); (4) papyri.

Present-day "<u>*textual criticism*</u>," founded chiefly by unbelievers, is glorified, not only by Roman Catholic leaders, by Protestant apostate leaders, by New

Evangelical leaders, but also by many Fundamentalist leaders. Examples of some of the Fundamentalist institutions that pay teachers who blindly follow unbelieving "*textual criticism*" are as follows:

(1) Bob Jones University;
(2) Detroit Baptist Theological Seminary;
(3) Central Baptist Seminary;
(4) Calvary Baptist Theological Seminary;
(5) Northland Baptist Bible College;
(6) Maranatha Baptist Bible College; and
(7) International Baptist College, to name only a few.

These institutions favor the apostate-founded Critical Greek New Testament texts variously called the Westcott/Hort Text, the Nestle/Aland Text, or the United Bible Societies Text. These same institutions also favor and sell in their bookstores such Bible versions based on these Greek texts as the New American Standard Version and the English Standard Version. It wouldn't surprise me if one or more of these schools will in the future espouse the New International Version as some of their graduates have done.

It is "*textual criticism*" that says it is all right for Christians that to **accept** the **8,000 changes** in the New Testament Greek Words of the Critical Text of Nestle/Aland 26 and 27 and **reject** the New Testament Greek Words underlying the King James Bible as printed in *Scrivener's Annotated Greek New Testament* (#1670 @ **$35.00** + **$6.00 S&H**). For a copy of these 8,000 changes, you should get Dr. Jack Moorman's *8,000 Differences Between the Critical Text and the Textus Receptus* (#3084 @ **$20.00** + **$6.00 S&H**). If you really want to see a preliminary examination of the manuscripts on both sides of these 8,000 differences, you should get Dr. Jack Moorman's 720 large-page study entitled *A Manuscript Digest of the New Testament--Preliminary Edition* (#3324 @ **$40.00** + **$8.00 S&H**).

Doubtful Differences Data

STATEMENT #198. (p. 298) Sproul is talking now about 8 differences in the Old Testament. He wrote: "*However, both Ben Chayim [sic] and Ben Asher are Masoretic texts. In truth, they only have eight differences in all the Old Testament.*"

COMMENT #198. I do not agree with Sproul on this point at all. I doubt whether Sproul has scanned the entire Ben Chayyim Hebrew Text into a computer and compared it with the already scanned Ben Asher Hebrew Text. Without having done this, he has only guess work to back up his statement. If he has scanned Ben Chayyim, I would like to buy a copy from him. I believe there are many more differences than eight. In 1906 and 1912, Rudolph Kittel used the same Hebrew Text as everyone else. It was the Ben Chayyim Text of Daniel Bomberg. Then, all of the sudden, in 1937 Kittel and/or his followers changed to the Ben Asher Hebrew Text. I do not believe Kittel and his followers would have made this change unless there were far more than eight differences between the two. One of the main differences is the addition of upwards of 20,000 to 30,000 critical footnotes which suggest changes in the Hebrew Words in the Text.

Sproul Denies "Preserved Words"

STATEMENT #199. (p. 300) "_God preserved his Word_ in the _abundance of manuscripts._"

COMMENT #199. Again Sproul states that "_God preserved his Word_. He denies the preservation of the Hebrew, Aramaic, and Greek Words, but only the "_Word_," by which he means **only** the "_ideas, thoughts, concepts, message, truth, or teachings._

> When Sproul talked about the "_abundance of manuscripts_, he never once has told his readers exactly where the Hebrew, Aramaic, and Greek **Words** are today. There are, as of this date, a total of **5,750 Greek manuscripts** plus **thousands of Hebrew manuscripts**. How many living people in this world:
>
> (1) know where all of these manuscripts are located;
> (2) has enough to money to travel around the world to find all of these;
> (3) has enough time in his lifetime to inspect carefully all of these;
> (4) knows how to read all of these; and
> (5) has enough intellect to determine which Hebrew, Aramaic, and Greek Words are the correct one?

This is a serious defect in Sproul's Bibliology. It that Christians of a solid and sure foundation for his Bible. Sproul's title of _God's Word Preserved_ is deceit to the nth degree since he doesn't really know if God's Words are "_preserved,_" and if so, he doesn't know **where** they are "_preserved._"

"Many Copies" of Bible Words

STATEMENT #200. (p. 300) "_Historically, too many copies existed too quickly for any man or council to ever gain control of every, or even most of the copies of the Word of God._"

COMMENT #200. That may be true, but the Gnostics of Alexandria, Egypt had enough important copies to pollute, and they did pollute them. These polluted Gnostic copies of the Vatican and Sinai manuscripts and others like them are the basis of the Critical Text today. These manuscripts number less than 1% of those in existence today.

Praise God that many other Christians all over the world were not Gnostics. They had unperverted and undoctored copies that were pure. Over 99% of the manuscripts that we now have are of these good kinds of manuscripts.

"Textual Criticism" Is Dangerous

STATEMENT #201. (p. 300) *"However, textual variation from geographic distribution and multiplicity of manuscripts, hence <u>textual criticism, is the observable method God has used</u> to insure the accuracy and permanency of His <u>Word</u>."*

COMMENT #201. Sproul is completely wrong when he stated that "<u>textual criticism is the observable method God has used</u>."

In point of fact, both unbelievers and some believers using so-called "*textual criticism*" have been used of the Devil (not God) to foist upon the Christian world corrupt Words rather than the true <u>Words</u> of God.

Notice that Sproul again is only interested in the "<u>Word</u>" of God, not the "<u>Words</u>" of God. I have explained the difference in these two terms many times above.

"God's Way" Is Always Best

STATEMENT #202. (p. 301) One of Sproul's headings was: *"Is <u>God's Way</u> Better than the '<u>KJV-only</u>' Way?"*

COMMENT #202. As I have said many times earlier, I am not '<u>KJV Only</u>.' This is a smear term to tie me and others into the false Ruckmanite position. Sproul thinks that his mistaken and faulty way is "<u>God's Way</u>." Such humility!

STATEMENT #203. (p. 301), *"<u>God's way of textual preservation</u> is better than the man-invented history of the 'KJV-only' movement that places a perfect version in the hands of one person or group controlled by the church hierarchy susceptible to additions and deletions at the whim of leaders."*

COMMENT #203. "<u>God's way of textual preservation</u>" involves, not the Ruckmanite "<u>perfect version</u>" or translation, but perfect preservation of the original Hebrew, Aramaic, and Greek Words. Sproul doesn't believe we have any of these, but I certainly do. He thinks we should have endless searches for the Words and never stop searching, thus never having a sure foundation of our Bible. This is his leaning toward the godless method of endless "<u>textual criticism</u>" which he loves.

"Enshrine" the"Fundamental Fathers"?

STATEMENT #204. (p. 302) *"Enshrining one of <u>the many scores of TRs</u> or one of the multiple revisions of the <u>OKJV as the inerrant, infallible,</u>*

inspired and only 'exact' Word for the English-speaking people is not promised by God, witnessed in any other language, or historically believed by the Separatist Fundamental Fathers."

COMMENT #204. How can Sproul commit such a lie as this, stating to his readers that there are "*many scores of TRs*?" A "*score*" is twenty. "*many scores*" would be forty, sixty, eighty and more. He would be hard pressed to find even twenty, even including all of the various editions of the TR's, but forty, sixty, eighty or more which would be "*many scores,*" has no basis in fact. Sproul's documentation is a total failure here, as in many other places in this book.

I do not agree with Sproul's referring to the "*OKJV as the inerrant, infallible, inspired and only 'exact' Word.*" This is Ruckmanism. If he wants to battle Peter Ruckmnan, why doesn't he write a book on this instead of presenting to his readers that I, and many others like me, hold to the Ruckman position on the King James Bible.

Notice Sproul's return to the worship of his "*Separatist Fundamental Fathers*" once again. His foundation is the writings of fallible men rather than the **Words** of an infallible God. Do they have the last word of truth? No, of course not!

"Text-Types" Are False

STATEMENT #205. (p. 308) Sproul lists four "*Text-types geographically*":

1. *Western (Italy)*
2. *Caesarean (Israel)*
3. *Byzantine (Turkey or Asia Minor and Greece)*
4. *Alexandrian (North Africa.*

COMMENT #205. Sproul believes in Westcott and Hort's "*Text-types*" which, in reality do not exist. This fallacy has been refuted clearly in the books of Dean John William Burgon. My readers should order the Revision Revised (#611 @ $25.00 + $5.00 S&H) and see the proof that all of the surviving manuscripts are like orphan children with no provable connection with one another and certainly not grouped as "*Text-types.*"

The reason for the invention of the false "*Text-types*" is so that the less than 1% of the evidence can win the battle against the more than 99% of the manuscript evidence. In the three so-called "*Text-types*" of "Western, Caesarean, and Alexandrian," there are found only about 45 manuscripts which form less than 1% of the manuscripts involved. When these false and doctored manuscripts agree together against the over 99% of the evidence, by the use of "*Text-types,*" they win by a vote of three to one. What a dishonest way to win a debate (with lies and falsehoods)!

Many Critical Text Variations

STATEMENT #206. (p. 312) Sproul, with approval, quotes Lewis Sperry Chafer who quotes Manley as follows: *"Only about 400 of 100,000 or 150,000 variations materially affect the sense. Of these, again not more than about fifty are really important for some reason or other; even of these fifty not one affects an article of faith or precept of duty, which is not abundantly substantiated or sustained by other and undoubted passages, or by the whole tenor of Scriptural teachings."*

COMMENT #206. The "*100,000 or 150,000 variations*" that Sproul quotes here represent the wide variations in the Critical Text itself. Dr. Jack Moorman has shown that there about 8,000 variations between the Critical Text and the Textus Receptus Words underlying the King James Bible. (See *8,000 Differences*, **BFT #3084 @ $20.00 + $7.00 S&H**).

Sproul is wrongly trying to persuade his readers that these 8,000 differences do not "*materially affect the sense.*" You have only to read the passages from Matthew through Revelation to see how wrong Sproul is on this.

Then, Sproul seeks to downplay doctrinal differences by saying that "*not one affects an article of faith or precept of duty, which is not abundantly substantiated.*" In another book by Dr. Jack Moorman (*Early Manuscripts, Church Fathers, and the Authorized Version* (**BFT #3230 @ $20.00 + $7.00 S&H**) on pages 119 to 312 of this 456-page hardback book, Dr. Moorman catalogs 356 doctrinal passages where the Critical Text is in error doctrinally. Of these 356, there are many that are taught in no other place. I want every doctrine to appear in every place it is supposed to occur. I don't want to traipse around page after page in the Bible to find the doctrine. Doctrine should be where it is supposed to be in every single place. We should not use the Bible versions based on the Critical Text because they do not have all the doctrines. Doctrine is disturbed and it is not "*abundantly substantiated*" elsewhere. One example of this is found in 1 Timothy 3:16 which, in the King James Bible, states that "*God was manifest in the flesh.*" This doctrine has been removed in the Critical Text and those versions based upon it. It is not mentioned by them in any other place. Faith is disturbed. This is the only place in the New Testament that we see "*God was manifest in the flesh.*"

"Translational Sense" Differences

STATEMENT #207. (pp. 311-312, footnote #71) Sproul quotes with approval George Ricker Berry's apparatus as follows: *"Only four to six hundred variant readings seriously affect the translational sense of any passage in the entire New Testament."*

COMMENT #207. That is Sproul's and Berry's opinion as to how many "*variant readings*" do "*seriously affect the translational sense of any* *passage*." I do not share this opinion.   If you examine every one of the differences between the Critical Text and the Textus Receptus Words underlying the King James Bible (as I have done) you might differ with these gentlemen also. I urge my readers to secure Dr. Jack Moorman's book, *8,000 Differences Between he Words Underlying the Modern Versions and the Words of the New Testament Greek in the King James Bible* (BFT #3084 @ $20.00 + $7.00 S&H).

In another book by Dr. Jack Moorman (*Early Manuscripts, Church Fathers, and the Authorized Version* (BFT #3230 @ $20.00 + $7.00 S&H) on pages 119 to 312 of this 456-page hardback book, Dr. Moorman catalogs **356 doctrinal passages** which "*seriously affect the translational sense of any passage*."

Sproul Denies "Biblical Preservation"

STATEMENT #208. (p. 313) "*Would Biblical preservation make more sense if God preserved his Word the way those of the 'KJV-only' camp claim? The question is immaterial. God did not preserve the Bible for modern Christians the way those of that persuasion theorize.*"

COMMENT #208. Again, Sproul is lumping me and others into this Ruckman camp by using his libelous term "***KJV-only***" to include us. In "***Biblical preservation***," God promised to preserve His **Words**, not only his "***Word***" by which Sproul means only His "*ideas, thoughts, concepts, message, truth, or teachings.*" I am in a camp with the Dean Burgon Society and the Bible For Today Ministry and others who detest the Ruckmanite "***KJV-only***" label used to libel and smear us. I refuse to be pigeon-holed into this '***KJV-only***' camp, which is the Peter Ruckman camp. The Lord Jesus said, "*Heaven and earth shall pass away, but my Words shall not pass away*" (Matthew 24:35; Mark 13:31; Luke 21:33). The Lord Jesus Christ promised to preserve His **Words** in all three of the above verses. I believe He has done this.

"In Heaven" Is Not An "Error"

STATEMENT #209. (p. 313) ". . . *Thomas Strouse, who would like Christians to **believe that the KJV is in error** and that '**in Heaven**' should really be translated '**by Heaven**.' Strouse's position is quite a strange position from one who believes 'In the KJV is the Word of God in the English language.*'"

COMMENT #209. Sproul gives a false twist in his charge that Dr. Strouse wants us to "***believe that the KJV is in error***." He never wrote that or said that.

If Sproul knows anything about the Hebrew language (and I do not know if he does or does not), he would know that the preposition "BETH" can equally be translated "*in*" or "*by*." Therefore, "***by Heaven***" is correct and "***in Heaven***" is also correct.

Singapore "Bible Presbyterian" Division

STATEMENT #210. (p. 314, footnote #79) *"In Singapore, a tremendous division is taking place over the issue among the Bible Presbyterians. The senior leader and founder pastor of the movement was forced out by those who are younger. D. A. Waite has had tremendous influence in Singapore among these 'young Turks.' Satan rejoices and the Sprit is quenched."*

COMMENT #210. Sproul has reversed this problem. It sounds like I had *"tremendous influence"* among the *"young Turks"* who were the *"younger"* people who *"forced out"* the *"senior leader"* in Singapore. On the contrary, I am on the same side as the *"senior leader"* and the *"younger"* or *"young Turks."* Sproul just doesn't know what he is talking about in this case as in other cases.

Those who take a pro-Bob Jones University false position in favor of the Critical Text forced Dr. Timothy Tow out of his church. He has now begun another church. Two younger leaders (Dr. Jeffrey Khoo and Dr. Quek) are following this *"senior leader"* and did not *"force him out."*

> **Dr. Timothy Tow and the Far Eastern Bible College and Seminary are standing true to the preservation of the Hebrew, Aramaic, and Greek Words underlying the King James Bible. The BJU followers in Singapore deny and oppose this position.**

Our Bible Position Is Not "Cultic"

STATEMENT #211. (p. 315) One of Sproul's section titles is: *"Are there Similarities Between KJV-onlyism and Modern Cults?"* Sproul wrote: *"Many of Separatism's leaders view with grave concern the insipid __cultic tendency__ of the 'KJV-only' movement."*

COMMENT #211. If Sproul limited his *"__KJV-only movement__"* to Peter Ruckman and his followers, yes, it certainly has a *"__cultic tendency__."* This would be honest and aboveboard. But Sproul is neither honest or aboveboard. He is dishonest in his reckless charges. He includes me and others who agree with me as having a *"__cultic tendency__."* This is a libelous, slanderous, and dishonest charge and I resent it strongly.

The Worship of "Separatist Fathers"

STATEMENT #212. (p. 315) *"Cult-like criticism of __the Separatist Fathers__ is infecting some quarters of the 'KJV-only' movement as self-anointed experts __attack godly men concerning their views of the transmission of the Text__. The aforementioned __cult leaders__ became the only source of truth to their followers by claiming that everyone else is deceived."*

102 A Critical Answer to God's Word Preserved

> **COMMENT #212.** It is certainly lamentable that Sproul is so defensive of "_the Separatist Fathers_." Are they all impeccable? Are they as the Lord Jesus Christ Himself--absolutely perfect? Could they not have made mistakes? For a Fundamentalist Baptist to worship frail human beings like they were the Pope of Rome is disgusting. Sproul's brain apparently has stopped thinking and learning beyond the conclusions of these men who wrote _the Fundamentals_ in 1915. This is obscurantism at its worst.

We must not be bound by the views of any man. If that is the case why not go all the way back with the early church fathers and say if they believe this then we can't believe anything else. If some of these men were Amillennialists, do we have to be Amillennialists? What if some of these men were five-point Calvinists do we have to be five-point Calvinists? Why is Sproul trying to tell us that the beliefs of these "_Separatist Fathers_" are the only beliefs we can believe and nothing else? Though there are many things with which we would agree, there are also others we would disagree with. We must be given this right to disagree. Sproul, from his all-powerful, all-knowing high tower denies us this right. I thought that as a Baptist Sproul would go to the Scriptures alone to get our doctrines. The Bible must be the exclusive foundation for our beliefs, faith, and doctrines. Sproul should know this. Then Sproul likens me and others that he smears with the epithet of "_KJV-only_" to such characters as "_Joseph Smith_" and even "_Jim Jones_." He implies that I am one of the "_cult leaders_." What is my sin which deserves such a smear term? I believe that God has preserved His original Bible Words in the Hebrew, Aramaic, and Greek Words underlying the King James Bible. Does this equal the heresies of "Joseph Smith" and "Jim Jones"?

Sproul also says of me and others who agree with me that we "_attack godly men concerning their views of the transmission of the Text_." I do not "_attack godly men_," but I certainly do attack "_their views of the transmission of the Text_" when they espouse the Westcott/Hort, Nestle/Aland, United Bible Societies Critical Text and the textual criticism that leads them to these deplorable texts.

We Aren't "Joseph Smith"&"Jim Jones"

STATEMENT #213. (p. 316) Sproul seeks to prove that "_KJV-only_" people are all members of a "_cult_." As such he says this applies: "_Destroy the Past to Re-create the Future._" Then Sproul says: "_Joseph Smith did this. Jim Jones did this._ PCC [Pensacola Christian College] _in their videos with Letis basically say,_ 'B. B. Warfield and his followers were dupes of the satanically wicked Westcott and Hort, thus all _our Fundamentalist Fathers_ are infected and wrong."

COMMENT #213. I do not "_destroy the Past_." I keep what is true from the "_past_" and reject what is untrue. I keep what is true from the present and future and reject what is untrue. I and others who agree with my position do not fall into Sproul's cult basket.

When Sproul says that "_Joseph Smith did this. Jim Jones did this,_" Sproul is libeling and slandering decent Fundamentalist brethren who disagree with him on the Hebrew, Aramaic, and Greek Words underlying the King James Bible and on the King James Bible itself.

When he talks about Pensacola Christian College, Sproul is forced to make up his so-called "_facts._" He says that this school and Letis "_basically say._" He does not have a quotation. If he had one, he would have quoted it. So, in order to smear and lie about the situation, he had to invent his "_facts._" What a shameless action to take by such an educated Fundamentalist leader!

Sproul repeats his defense of and even worship of "_our Fundamentalist Fathers._" Is this not a form of human idolatry? Doesn't he think that they made even one little tiny error in any of their lengthy articles?

STATEMENT #214. (p. 316) Sproul again seeks to prove that "_KJV-only_" people are all members of a "_cult._" As such he says this statement applies: "_Others are similar to us, but they are not exactly pure so do not fellowship with them._" Then Sproul says: "_This is extremely cultic and it is how Jim Jones got so many to drink Kool-Aid. Meanwhile, godly historical fundamentalists use the TR (but prefer the Majority Text) and Masoretic Text, while taking the same view on the means and location of God's preserved Word as 400 years of Separatists and Baptists, yet those Fundamentalists are barely tolerated and certainly not embraced by fellow independent Baptists who adhere to KJV-onlyism._"

COMMENT #214. Sproul uses the words, "_do not fellowship with them_" to mean that we who stand for the Textus Receptus and defend it do not want to "_fellowship_" with the Critical Text people. I have never denied a request to come to speak on this subject at Bob Jones University, or at his school, International Baptist College in Tempe, Arizona. But the shoe is on the other foot. It is the Westcott/Hort Critical Text people who treat us Textus Receptus people as "_heretics._"

See **STATEMENT #172** above for the reference for Sproul's own group, the Fundamental Baptist Fellowship wanting our men to be "_rejected._" This smacks of pure hypocrisy on Sproul's part.

The "_Jim Jones_" and the "_Kool-Aid_" reference to his fellow Fundamentalists is reprehensible. Again, he exalts human beings above the Bible by his worship of the conclusions of "_400 years of Separatists and Baptists._" Sproul prefers to stay in a rut of 400 years and admit that these men have researched all the facts and there is nothing new to discover in textual matters.

Original "Words" Not Translators' Words

STATEMENT #215. (p. 317) *"Now compare Brown's position in the founding documents of the 'KJV-only' movement to that of Khoo, Waite, or Cloud and their current reasoning. When presented with the scores of differences between TRs, their methodology to identify the perfectly preserved Word is to agree with the word the 1611 translators chose."*

COMMENT #215. It is not to agree with "*the word the 1611 translators chose*," but to the Traditional and Received Hebrew, Aramaic, and Greek Words underlying the King James Bible. These Words have been believed by the saints from the Apostolic Time to the present. They are good enough for me. Which are the "*perfectly preserved Words*" for Sproul? Let him bring them out, if he has any, and we can discuss them. He doesn't have any. That is a sad state of affairs--to have a Fundamental Baptist Pastor in leadership of a Fundamental Baptist College without any "*perfectly preserved Words*" to teach and preach.

The "Eclectic Text" Not "Eclectic"

STATEMENT #216. (p. 317) *"'KJV-only' advocates like Cloud have pounded 'every word is perfect in the KJV' and attacked the eclectic Text position for not knowing 'where the Bible is' so hard that when they are finally confronted with scores of differences in the TRs they have the same problem that they asserted their opponents have."*

COMMENT #216. I do not use the term "*perfect*" in the phrase "*every word is perfect in the KJV*." Only God is "*perfect*." I use the word "*accurate*" and yet I don't believe the KJB is "*imperfect*." However, in the area of the Apocrypha, the KJB translators were most "*imperfect*." They never should have included it in their 1611 KJB.

Sproul is not correct when he wrote about those who follow the Textus Receptus, "*they have the same problem that they asserted their opponents have*." It is not the "*same problem*." Critical Texts have several thousands of differences among them, many of them major. Textus Receptus Texts have only a few hundred and these few are minor.

The Scrivener's TR Is the "Right One"

STATEMENT #217. (p. 317) *"Which TR is the right one? They did not reconsider their a priori, that God had preserved every word of the autographs in the KJV, Scrivener's TR, or the Masoretic Text they just went further out on a limb toward Ruckman's position."*

COMMENT #217. I do not believe, nor do others who agree, that God "*preserved every word of the autographs in the KJV.*" This is pure Ruckmanism and yet Sproul does not differentiate between those who believe this and those who believe, as I do, that "*every word of the autographs*" is preserved in the Scrivener's TR and the Masoretic Words underlying the King James Bible. That is **not** Ruckmanism, and Sproul should make this clear.

> **We do not take Ruckman's position that God breathed out English words.**

As to Sproul's question, "*Which TR is the right one?*" For me, it is Beza's 5th edition of 1598 as modified slightly (in only 190 places according to Scrivener). This is only 0.14% of the whole.

Proper Interpretation of "Passages"

STATEMENT #218. (p. 318) Sproul is talking about Dr. Kent Brandenburg, "*This is exactly what Brandenburg does with fideistic faith in his recent 'KJV-only' book.* [Brandenburg is not a Ruckmanite, but Sproul is using this smear term to refer to him.] *He places his faith not in the Bible, but rather his interpretation of several passages which have never been understood that way in 400 years of Baptist thought.*"

COMMENT #218. Sproul tells another lie when he says, "*He places his faith not in the Bible.*" He does use "*several passages*" which are very clear about verbal plenary preservation of the Words of God. Some of these "*passages*" are Matthew 24:35; Mark 13:31; Luke 21:33; and Matthew 5:18. Once again, Sproul goes back to "*400 years of Baptist thought*" rather than the literal interpretation of such verses as these.

> **Sproul wants to freeze all Bible exegesis with what the 400-year-old "*Baptist thought*" believed.**

He should get his head "*out of the sand*" as they say and not be a Neanderthal in Biblical exegesis.

Sproul's "Different Definitions"

STATEMENT #219. (p. 318) Sproul names another technique of his kind of "KJV-only" people: "*Use the same words as others, but give them different definitions.*" Sproul then quoted his former senior Pastor: "*Dr. Singleton used to say about Mormons, 'They have the same vocabulary, but a different dictionary.' An example of this technique in the 'KJV-only' controversy comes from the 'Landmark Anchor--December, 2004.' The author of the article [asked], 'When did the idea begin that God has preserved the Bible?'*"

COMMENT #219. Sproul is talking about using the "same words," but "*give them different definitions.*" This is exactly what Sproul himself does as well as Bob Jones University, Detroit Baptist Seminary, Central Baptist Seminary, Calvary Baptist Seminary and their Fundamentalist cohorts. They say they believe in the "*preservation of the Word of God*" but use "different definitions" for "*Word*" of God. They don't mean "*Words*" of God, but only the "*ideas, thoughts, concepts, message, truth, or teachings.*" This is a masterful use of doing what the Mormons do, they use a "*different dictionary*." What a hypocrisy and sham! Sproul's own book title, *God's Word Preserved* is an example of his use of a "*different dictionary*" for "*Word*" and for "*Preserved.*" They prostitute those terms and re-define them to their own twisted purposes. This is hypocrisy and duplicity. All I can mention is the old saying which is so true in this case, "*It takes one to know one.*" When the Bible uses the term "*Word*"of God, the Bible is referring to the "*Words*" of God, as in Psalm 119:11, for example, which says, "*Thy Word have I hid in mine heart, that I might not sin against Thee.*"

As for the question Sproul quotes: "*When did the idea begin that God has preserved the Bible?* The answer is simple. This idea began in the Bible which promised that "*God has preserved the Bible.*" By the "*Bible,*" I mean the original Hebrew, Aramaic, and Greek Words. Sproul and his friends deny that God has done this. I and my friends affirm that God has done this.

False Re-Definition of Bible Terms

STATEMENT #220. (p. 320) "*Brandenburg changes the definition of the term preservation and applies it to the TR of Scrivener as being 'complete, inerrant protection and general accessibility of every writing of the Bible, the sixty-six books of the Old and New Testaments, for every generation of believers.' This is a completely new way of defining three key terms: preservation, Masoretic Text, and Textus Receptus.*"

COMMENT #220. I am sure that Sproul has misquoted Brandenburg about the "*TR of Scrivener*" as applying to the "*Old*" Testament. I am sure that he referred to the Masoretic Text to refer to the "*Old*" Testament and the "*TR of Scrivener*" to refer to the New Testament. It is Sproul and his followers who have a "*completely new way of defining*" the terms "*preservation, Masoretic Text, and Textus Receptus.*" Brandenburg is specific in each of these definitions. Sproul is not. Nowhere does Sproul define what he means by these three terms. As I have said above, except for about 190 places (only about 0.14% of the Greek New Testament), the King James Bible translators used Beza's 5th Edition, 1598. All of these Words are contained in Scrivener's Greek New Testament.

STATEMENT #221. (p. 320) "*Using familiar theological words or historical figures but attaching different meanings to them than originally* *intended* has always been the *methodology of cults* to seduce unsuspecting people."

COMMENT #221. As I have said before, Sproul and his Fundamentalist Critical Text and New Versions friends have written the book on "*Using familiar theological words*" but "*attaching different meanings to them than originally intended*." This is pure hypocrisy on Sproul's part. As I have said before, his book title, *God's Word Preserved*, is a case in point. He doesn't believe "*Word*" means Hebrew, Aramaic, and Greek "*Words*" in which our Bible was written. He therefore does not believe that God has preserved these "*Words*." Yet his title appears to state this. He has used "*familiar theological words*" ("*Word*" and "*preserved*) and yet has "*attached different meanings to them than originally intended*." This is his own definition of the "*methodology of cults*." Sproul is guilty as charged.

STATEMENT #222. (p. 320) "The **'KJV-only' position** uses orthodox words: inerrancy, preservation, inspired, etc., but as history reveals neither group attaches the same **definitions** to these terms **as Separatists have historically**."

COMMENT #222. Sproul is contrasting what he calls the "*KJV-only" position* " with the "*cults*" like Joseph Smith and the Mormons. Why should people today necessarily define these terms "*as Separatists have historically*"? Here is Sproul's man-worship once again. I repeat, when things of the past are true, we can accept them. When they are false, we must reject them. Sproul apparently wants to accept both the true things and the false things of the past if they came from the pens of the "*Separatists*."

> I am a "*Separatist*." Sproul is a "*Separatist*." But neither of us "*Separatists*" or any other "*Separatists*" are perfect and without errors. We should take the position of the Bible and not the position of the "*Separatists*" who might not be standing on the Bible's Words.

As far as changing "*definitions*" of terms, when Michael Sproul says that he believes in Bible "*preservation*," he does not really believe this. He does not believe in the "*preservation*" of the original Hebrew, Aramaic, and Greek Words. This is hypocrisy, duplicity, and confusion.

Wrongly Fusing "Ruckman" & Waite

STATEMENT #223. (p. 321-322) Sproul's heading is: "*Is the rhetoric of many in the 'KJV-only' leadership Christ-Honoring?*" He then writes: "*Riplinger, Ruckman, Waite. Yarnell, and Grady--all of these 'KJV-only' protagonists have made strong denunciations of godly Fundamentalist leaders in their writings.*"

COMMENTS #223. Notice Sproul's erroneous link up of the names, "*Ruckman, Waite*." Sproul calls us both "*'KJV-only' protagonists*." Do you see why I divorce myself from this smear/Ruckmanite term of *"KJV-only"?* Sproul knows full well that I am totally opposed to Ruckman and that he is totally opposed to me. If he doesn't know this, he should before writing such a book. And yet he links Ruckman with me as though we're on the same side in this battle for the Bible.

I believe that Peter Ruckman is a heretic and an apostate on the Bible issue. Peter Ruckman believes that God breathed-out the King James Bible (including the italics). That is heretical. That is apostate as far as Bibliology is concerned. I am absolutely incensed that Sproul would put my name right after Peter Ruckman and would yoke me up with this man. This is libelous and slanderous.

My Two-Pronged "Writing Style"

STATEMENT #224. (p. 322) *"Waite's pen drips with harsh rhetoric. Is their writing style better described by Galatians 5:19-21 or Galatians 5:22-23? Sadly, some Christians reveal their own sinful appetites by their enjoyment of such a harsh and carnal writing style as these men unleash their pens on other godly Christians."*

COMMENT #224. By Sproul's use of the phrase, *"their writing style,"* he includes *"Riplinger, Ruckman, Waite, Yarnell, and Grady."* I don't have to answer for the others mentioned, but I can answer for his charge that *"Waite's pen drips with harsh rhetoric."* Sproul, of course, is entitled to his opinion about my *"rhetoric."* He can call it *"harsh and carnal writing style"* if he wishes.

My writing and rhetoric is characterized by two things: **(1)** a strong defense and advocacy of Biblical truth, and **(2)** a strong exposure and censure of Biblical error. Those who are in Biblical error do not like either strong exposure or censure. To them it is considered *"harsh and carnal."*

My friend, my writing style is used on those things that are wrong, unscriptural, or apostate in doctrine and nature. As far as my *"rhetoric,"* when Sproul or those from other fundamental schools, in addition to his school where he is the chairman of the board, will mistranslate Scripture and redefine words such as Bible Preservation when he doesn't believe God's Words are preserved I will be bold and clear in my speaking and writing. I will continue to be and bold against misinformation, misquotation, sin, and wickedness just like the Lord Jesus Christ Himself, and like the Apostle Paul. Paul asked the Galatians:

"Am I therefore become your enemy, because I tell you the truth?" (Galatians 4:16)

I am sure Peter did not appreciate Paul when he *"withstood him to the face"* when he was to be *"blamed."*

"But when Peter was come to Antioch, I withstood him to the face, because he was to be blamed." (Galatians 2:11)

Sproul and his friends do not like it when I point out their misquotations, the errors, and especially when they connect me to the Ruckmanites and the "**_KJV-only_**" movement. I stand in truth for godly things and I am against anything that smacks of error such as this book of Sproul's.

What is Sproul's writing style and "**_rhetoric_**"? He ties me in repeatedly with Peter Ruckman and with his "**_KJV-only_**" title. In so doing, he refuses to separate those who stand for the Hebrew, Aramaic, and Greek Words underlying the King James Bible, as well as the King James Bible from those who take the King James Bible as superseding the original Bible Words. This is inexcusable. It is poor scholarship. It is slanderous, libelous, untruthful, false, and scurrilous. You'll have to pardon me, but I am not fond of Sproul's _"rhetoric."_ In this battle for our Bible, anyone who is twisting the truth and making up lies I will expose. Talk about "**_harsh_**" words, Sproul has written a whole book using them. Sproul compares me (and others) to Joseph Smith and Jim Jones and his use of poisoned Kool-Aid to kill his followers. This is vicious.

> As far as the false charge that I and others he listed "**_unleash their pens on other godly Christians,_**" let me say this. Though this cannot be said of "Ruckman" whom Sproul lists, I do not "**_unleash my pen_**" on "**_godly Christians,_**" but on any false teachings or unscriptural positions or beliefs that might be held by "**_godly Christians._**" There is a great deal of difference between these two things.

Our "Position" Is Not "New"

STATEMENT #225. (p. 323) *"Perhaps these authors cannot admit their position is new because they might be obligated to write in a more Christian manner."*

COMMENT #225. By Sproul's use of the words, "*these authors*, he is tying me in with the heretic, Peter Ruckman. This is what people sometimes call "*dirty pool*." Why doesn't Sproul take the time to subdivide each of the five authors he has listed and answer each one separately? Of course, that would take more of his time. He couldn't possibly take the time to be fair. He must be unfair and so he throws me into the Ruckman pot and blackens my good name with his soiled name. Sproul knows just how to besmirch good and godly Fundamentalists with whom he disagrees. Just link them to rowdy Ruckman, and it gets his disrespectable job done.

As to Sproul's false charge that "*their position is new*," on Bible preservation (which teaches that the original Hebrew, Aramaic, and Greek Words have been preserved) is as old as the New Testament and the Words of the Lord Jesus Christ in three of the four Gospels. "

"Heaven and earth shall pass away, but_my words shall not pass away." (Matthew 24:35; Mark 13:31; Luke 21:33)

This the verbal plenary preservation view is the OLD view taught by the Lord Jesus Christ Himself. It is accepted by me and other Fundamentalists. It is rejected by Sproul and other Fundamentalists.

"Fundamentalists" Not Called "Infidels"

STATEMENT #226. (p. 323) *"Suddenly, the leaders realize that the 'infidels' they deride are Fundamentalism's Fathers."*

COMMENT #226. Notice once again that Sproul ties five names together, including "*Ruckman*" and "*Waite*."

I have never called "*Fundamentalism's Fathers*" by the name of "*infidels*." This is a spurious and erroneous charge. I do not agree with their various positions in favor of Westcott and Hort's Critical Greek Text, or with their advocacy of the English Revised Version of 1881, but they certainly were not "*infidels*."

The "Forefathers" Were Dupes of W/H

STATEMENT #227. (p. 323) *"Separatism's godly forefathers are often viewed even more negatively as dupes of the sinister forces of Westcott and Hort as well as Darwin."*

COMMENT #227. As Sproul knows very well, the greater number of the writers of *the Fundamentals* of 1915 were followers of "*Westcott and Hort*" and their deceptively false Greek New Testament Text. This is why they quote repeatedly from the 1881 English Revised Version edited by Anglican churchmen led by "*Westcott and Hort*."

I Do Not Use "Perfect" For KJB

STATEMENT #228. (p. 325) *"Further, if Christ tarries, the generation that is hearing 'every word in your KJV is the perfect one' will never consider another good formal equivalent translation, not now not in one thousand years."*

COMMENT #228. Sproul would be hard-pressed to find any place in my speaking or writing where I have said that "*every word in your KJV is the perfect one*." I use the word "*perfect*" for God alone and the things that God does. I say that the original Hebrew, Aramaic, and Greek Words underlying the King James Bible are "*perfect*" Words, inspired Words, and preserved Words. The King James Bible's translation of those Words is the only accurate one that we have today.

Sproul knows that it is growing more unlikely as time passes that there will ever be another English translation based on these same preserved Words and done with such great accuracy. Such a translation would have to be superior in texts, superior in translators, superior in translation technique, and superior in theology like the King James Bible presently is.

CHAPTER EIGHT: GOD COMMUNICATES THROUGH SPIRIT-FILLED LEADERS (pp. 329-344)

Two Standards of Correct Translation

STATEMENT #229. (p. 329) This begins Sproul's Chapter 8. the title is: *"God Communicates Through Spirit-Filled Leaders--Fundamentalism's Real Issue."* Under this heading, Sproul said: *"But there are people who fanatically insist that the King James Version was <u>perfectly translated with no errors.</u>"*

> **COMMENT #229.** I do not believe the King James Bible has any what I call *"translational errors."* The King James translators had accurate translations from their underlying Hebrew, Aramaic and Greek manuscripts. Those words were given at least one accurate English meaning. There may have been three or four other meanings, but the King James translators picked at least one of the correct meanings.

As far as the rules of syntax or grammar, though there might have been other rules they could have followed, the translators followed at least one of the proper rules. I do not use terms such as perfect, inerrant, or infallible when referring to the King James Bible. Those terms I reserve for God's original Hebrew, Aramaic, and Greek Words and the copies of these preserved Words underlying the King James Bible. I believe the King James Bible is the only accurate English translation because it was translated from the proper Hebrew, Aramaic and Greek Words.

One very serious error about the original 1611 King James Version was its inclusion of the Apocrypha. According to an Internet article in **ASSORTMENT** entitled *"The Apocrypha, Canon & Bible,"* Speaking about the Apocrypha books, the article stated: *"They were dropped from the King James Version in 1796."* If this date is correct (and I have read of earlier dates), they should not have waited so long before removing these heretical documents.

Greek MSS Do Divide "God's People"

STATEMENT #230. (p. 331) *"John R. Rice wrote in December of 1972 an article titled, 'Why Divide God's People About <u>Greek Manuscripts</u> They Cannot Know About.'"*

COMMENT #230. In a booklet in 1979, John R. Rice is quoted as saying the following:

> "<u>The differences in the translations are so minor</u>, so insignificant, that we can be sure <u>not a single doctrine</u>, not a single <u>statement of fact</u>, not a single command or exhortation, has been missed in our translations." [As quoted in *Bible Translations* by Evangelist R. L. Sumner, p. 18, 1979]

> From this statement about "<u>the differences in the translations</u>" by John R. Rice, I am thoroughly convinced that, though he was good in other areas, he didn't have the faintest idea about the truth in the area of Bible "<u>translations</u>." The "<u>differences in the translations</u>" are not "<u>minor</u>." They are major because of the 8,000 differences in the Greek New Testament texts on which the translations are based. These differences amount to 356 doctrinal passages which are "<u>missed in our translations</u>." [See BFT #3084 and BFT #3230 as previously noted above]

Since Rice's words were so false in the area of "<u>translations</u>," I cannot take as believable his words here on "<u>Greek Manuscripts</u>." Just because Rice did not "<u>know about</u>" the "<u>Greek Manuscripts</u>," the evidences in many books are now available so that "<u>God's people</u>" can "<u>know about</u>" the issues involved and when they see the truth, they will want to be "<u>divided</u>" against the Critical Greek N.T. Text and stand for the preserved original Hebrew, Aramaic, and Greek Words underlying the King James Bible. Truth versus error is a subject that must "<u>divide God's people</u>." Without the victory of the truth of God's Words, error will continue from generation to generation.

I Don't Use "Perfection" For the KJB

STATEMENT #231. (p. 332) *"Considering how much attention from the pulpit <u>the 'perfection' of the KJV</u> receives in some churches, a visitor might think that the topic is the most important issue confronting Fundamentalism. (<u>People leave churches</u> thinking that the church no longer takes '<u>a fundamental position</u>' on the KJV issue; . . .)"*

COMMENT #231. On the subject of "<u>in the 'perfection' of the KJV</u>," I have said above that I use the term "accurate." I do not use such words as *"perfection," "perfect," "inspired," "infallible," "inerrant,"* and other terms wrongly used by Peter Ruckman and his followers for the King James Bible. I use every one of these words for God's original Hebrew, Aramaic, and

Greek Words which have been preserved in the Words underlying the King James Bible.

As far as why "*people leave churches*" because, in their opinion, these churches no longer take what they believe to be "*'a fundamental position'* on the Bible, let me say this. "What is wrong with this"? People "*leave churches*" for a number of reasons. Why should people not be free to go to a church, for instance, that not only uses but also defends the King James Bible. This is what our 𝕭𝖎𝖇𝖑𝖊 𝖋𝖔𝖗 𝕿𝖔𝖉𝖆𝖞 𝕭𝖆𝖕𝖙𝖎𝖘𝖙 𝕮𝖍𝖚𝖗𝖈𝖍 does each week. I left a church because they switched, after one hundred years, from the King James Bible to the New King James Version. This is our freedom as born-again Christians. Many people have left churches because of the new Bible versions they have started to use.

> **I have people write to me all the time and ask me where they can find a good Bible-believing church that stands for, preaches from, and defends the King James Bible, and its underlying Hebrew, Aramaic, and Greek Words. These churches are getting fewer and fewer because schools and pastors are ridiculing our King James Bible.**

While it is true that many Fundamentalist preachers and teachers use and defend the modern versions like the NASV, ERV, and even the NIV, their "*position*" is not a "*fundamental position*" because of the more than 356 doctrinal passages in the above versions which are not "*fundamental*." This is most inconsistent.

The Holy Spirit Needs the Right Bible

STATEMENT #232. (p. 336) "*More important than intellectual agreement on a particular KJV or TR revision is empowerment through moment-by-moment dependence on the Sprit's strength.*"

COMMENT #232. It is fine to walk by means of the Holy Sprit. It's important to be filled with the Spirit of God, but it is also important to know what the Words of God are. If a person does not know Hebrew, Aramaic and Greek, but he knows English, he can read the King James Bible and know that he is reading the Words of God in English. **The King James Bible is an accurate translation.** The Fundamentalists who don't believe that we have the preserved Words of God don't know where the Words of God are. God the Holy Spirit works through God's Words. Unfaithful versions hinder the Holy Spirit's "*empowerment.*"

Can "Pastors" Be Trusted on the Bible?

STATEMENT #233. (p. 340) Sproul calls the following, "*fearful words*": "*Can I trust my pastor if he does not subscribe to the 'right' phrase of doctrinal belief as found in the 'KJV-only' movement.*"

COMMENT #233. Again, Sproul uses the broad smear term, '"*KJV-only'" movement*" to refer to me and others who stand with me, rather than defining terms strictly and going after the followers of Peter Ruckman alone. If you stand for the King James Bible and its underlying Hebrew, Aramaic, and Greek Words, and your pastor disagrees, of course you should seek a church and a pastor that agrees with your position, if you can find one.

Why "Preach" From An Inferior Bible?

STATEMENT #234. (p. 343) *"Having established our position on this issue, our ministry will __continue to preach from the KJV__ while continuing to hold high the local church Baptist distinctives of the Tri-City Baptist Church, and championing the historical fundamentals of the faith."*

COMMENT #234. I fail to understand why Sproul is going to "__continue to preach from the KJV__" when he praises other English versions, condemns the Hebrew, Aramaic, and Greek Words underlying it, and knocks those of us who stand for it. This is the greatest hypocrisy of all. Why does he use something he does not defend?

APPENDIX ONE:
FIVE REASONS FOR WORD
VARIATION IN DIFFERENT
TRANSLATIONS
(pp. 345-358)

NASV/NKJV Not "Formal Equivalent"

STATEMENT #235. (pp. 345 and 348) Appendix #1 entitled: *"Five Reasons For Word Variation in Different Translations."* the subtitle is: *"Translation Style, Theological Bias, Original Language Text-type, Original Language Printed Text, and Language Developing."* Under *"Translation Style,"* Sproul listed as using *"Formal Equivalent"* style: *"OKJV, NKJV, NASB, ESV."*

COMMENT #235. I would agree with Sproul's classification of the *"OKJV"* as *"Formal Equivalent,"* but I would be careful about using that term for either the *"OKJV"* or the *"NASB."* In my analysis (**BFT #1442**) from Genesis through Revelation of the New King James Version (*"NKJV"*) I found **over 2,000 examples** of dynamic equivalency (adding Words, subtracting Words, or changing Words in other ways) rather than being a *"Formal Equivalent"* translation. In my analysis (**BFT #1494**) of the New American Standard Version (*"NASB"*) I found **over 4,000 examples** of dynamic equivalency (adding Words, subtracting Words, or changing Words in other ways) rather than being a *"Formal Equivalent"* translation.

No "Text-Types"

STATEMENT #236. (pp 350-352) Sproul has a heading called, *"Original Language Text Types."*

COMMENT #236. Sproul mentioned the *"Byzantine or Majority Text-type,* the *Western Text-type,* the *Caesarean Text-type,"* and the *"Alexandrian Text-type."*

These so-called *"Text-types"* do not exist. They are only imaginary items dreamed up by Bishop Westcott and Professor Hort. They were first mentioned in the Introduction to the Greek Text followed by the English Revised Version of 1881. There is no proof whatsoever that Greek manuscripts are genealogically related and in *"families."*

I agree with Dean John William Burgon who stated that all the Greek manuscripts are like *"orphaned children."* You don't know which manuscript goes with which family so how can you classify them as belonging with one another? The illustration that Dean Burgon used was like going into a cemetery with unmarked graves, and trying to prove who is related and who is not. You can't do this. So it is with these Greek manuscripts of the New Testament.

TR Not "Minority" of "Majority Text"

STATEMENT #237. (p. 351) *"In the Textus Receptus is <u>a minority strain of the Majority Text</u>. It agrees with it 99% of the time. The TR is not a <u>Text type</u>."*

COMMENT #237. In the first place, how can Sproul's so-called "*<u>Majority Text</u>*" be in any sense of the word be in the "*<u>Majority</u>*"? The Text that goes by that name of Hodges and Farstad was primarily based on Herman Von Soden's approximate 414 Greek manuscripts. Where did Sproul go to school that taught him 414 is a majority of 5,255? I would like to know where he was taught this kind of math.

In the second place, there is no such thing as "*<u>Text type</u>*." This is the purely hypothetical guesswork initiated by theological heretics Westcott and Hort in their *Introduction* to their 1881 false Greek Text. (Cf. **BFT #1304**). It is a sad thing when Fundamentalists have bought into this error in thinking about the Greek New Testament.

How can Sproul say the Textus Receptus is "*<u>a minority strain of the Majority Text</u>*"? The Traditional Text or the Textus Receptus, which underlies our King James Bible, is not a minority Text. According to Dr. Jack Moorman's analysis of the manuscripts current in 1967 (5,255 in all at that time), 5,210 of them (over 99% of them) support the Traditional Text. The engineers of the so-called "*<u>Majority Text</u>*" that Sproul believes in have lied about their manuscript authority.

KJB Not "Eclectic"

STATEMENT #238. (p. 352) *"<u>The KJV was an eclectic version</u> primarily based on <u>Beza's 1598 printed Greek TR Text</u>. It did not follow Beza's Text word for word."*

COMMENT #238. Sproul has told a blatant falsehood by saying that "*<u>the KJV was an eclectic version</u>*." To claim that the KJV was "*eclectic,*" would imply that it was loaded with different Greek sources throughout it. This is totally false. As Dr. Frederick Scrivener has pointed out (**BFT #1670 @ $35.00 + S&H**), there are only 190 passages out of over 140,000 Greek Words in the New Testament where the King James translators did not follow "**Beza's 1598 printed Greek TR Text**." This is only 0.14% deviation from Beza's 5th edition of 1598.

"Westcott and Hort's" Text Is Here

STATEMENT #239. (p. 353) Sproul's paragraph heading is "_Westcott and Hort (9000 Differences with the TR?)_ the footnote attached to this heading is #16 which states: "_This is a rough guess. No one whom I know uses this Text, so the number of differences is irrelevant at the practical level._"

COMMENT #239. As I have mentioned previously, Dr. Jack Moorman's book, _8,000 Differences Between the Critical Text and the Textus Receptus_ identifies 8,000 differences rather than 9,000 differences. That "_rough guess_" of Sproul is fairly close.

Perhaps Sproul doesn't "_know_" any of the editors of the NASV, the NIV, the ESV, the NRSV or other modern versions, but they are all basing their New Testaments (with only minor variations) on the "_Westcott and Hort_" Greek Text. The "Westcott and Hort" Greek Text is based on the Vatican ("B") and the Sinai (Aleph) manuscripts. So are the Critical Texts of Nestle/Aland and the United Bible Societies. As in geometry, two things that are equal to the same thing are equal to each other. So, the new versions, being based on the same general basic Critical Greek texts of Vatican and Sinai as the Westcott and Hort Text of 1881, are virtually equal with very few modifications. I have six or seven quotations to document this assertion. Here is one of the quotes taken from my own power-point presentations:

> "_In 1990, Dr. Kirk D. DiVietro, a Baptist Pastor who was then in New Jersey, wrote to Princeton's Dr. Bruce Metzger about how he and the other members of the Nestle-Aland and United Bible Societies Committees began their work on their New Testament Greek Texts. Dr. Metzger replied to him as follows:_
>
> "_WE TOOK AS OUR BASE AT the BEGINNING the TEXT OF WESTCOTT AND HORT (1881) and introduced changes as seemed necessary on the basis of MSS evidence._"

This documentation is found in Metzger's own handwriting in B.F.T. #2490-P, p. 272 in _the Dean Burgon Society (1978--1994) Messages From the 16th Annual Meeting, August, 1994._"

STATEMENT #240. (p. 353) "_Concerning Westcott and Hort's original word choices. . . . their Text is not used today except by scholars as a vehicle of comparison._"

COMMENT #240. This is completely misleading. As mentioned above, Dr. Bruce Metzger was on the committees that compiled both the Nestle/Aland Greek Text and the United Bible Societies Greek Text. He said that the Committee "**took as their base at the beginning the Text of Westcott and Hort (1881).**" This is why the Nestle/Aland and the United Bible Societies Text are identical with that of Westcott and Hort except in very few minor particulars.

STATEMENT #241. (p. 253) *"However, few, if any, textual scholars today accept all of Westcott and Hort word choices; therefore, this Text has many changes when compared with Westcott and Hort's Text."*

COMMENT #241. Sproul is wrong again in this statement. When he mentions "*this Text has many changes*," he is referring to the "*United Bible Society's 4th edition*" Critical Text. The changes are not "*many*" but few. Sproul is repeating the false party line of the Critical Text Fundamentalists in order to distance themselves from the doctrinal apostasy of Westcott and Hort.

The "Critical Text" Is Inferior

STATEMENT #242. (p. 353) *"All four views look to ancient Lectionaries, ancient versions, and quotations of Fathers; but because this view has less actual manuscript support it seems this position does that more than the others."*

COMMENT #242. Sproul is talking about the "*Critical or Eclectic Text*" in his major heading here. In point of fact, the Critical Text uses the "*ancient Lectionaries, ancient versions, and quotations of Fathers*" much less than the Traditional or Received Text position. If you look in the introductions and appendices of either the Nestle/Aland Text or the United Bible Societies Text, you will find a very small percentage of references to these three kinds of evidence compared to the abundance of such references in Dean John W. Burgon's many published works when defending the Traditional Received Greek Text.

"Majority" Text Not Textus Receptus

STATEMENT #243. (p. 353) *"The Majority or Byzantine Text* [this is the Text that Michael Sproul holds to] *has 1,838 differences from the Textus Receptus."*

COMMENT #243. That estimate is no doubt fairly close for the so-called "*Majority*" Text of either Hodges and Farstad or of Robinson and Pierpont. That is why I am opposed to that Text. According to Dr. Jack Moorman's excellent research, these so-called "*Majority*" texts were based on about only 414 manuscripts that Von Sodden used. See When the So-Called "Majority Text" Departs From the Textus Receptus (**BFT #1617** @ **$16.00** +

S&P). 414 manuscripts is certainly not anywhere near a "*majority*" of the 5,255 manuscripts available in 1967. Nobody on this earth has examined all the manuscripts that we have and they never will.

To say that the "*Majority*" Text is the same as the "*Byzantine*" Text is a falsehood. This is a twist of the Fundamentalists who worship the Critical Greek Text. In point of fact, the "*Byzantine*" Text is the same as the Traditional or Received Greek Text that numbers as of 1967 about 5,210 manuscripts. This is over 99% of the evidence we had in that year.

KJV 1611 Can Be Read Today

STATEMENT #244. (p. 354) Sproul wrote: "*Reading an original KJV 1611 is nearly impossible for twenty-first century America. . . . I have been reared to listen to the KJV, memorize from the KJV, preach from the KJV, and earned a B.A., M. Div., and D.Min., in schools that only use the KJV, yet I did not know the meaning of certain words in my translation. If I did not know these idiomatic expressions or archaic words, how could the modern 'ploughboy' know them? Did God write in Attic Greek and expect all of the early Christians to carry a dictionary with them so they could understand what God had said?*"

COMMENT #244. If Sproul would get a 1611 King James Bible with the updated spelling and the proper script he can read it and understand it. If this man still does not understand the King James Bible, I would recommend he get a copy of the *Defined King James Bible*. The uncommon words are defined accurately in the footnotes. If Sproul's church people do not understand some of the words in the King James Bible, they should also get a copy of the *Defined King James Bible*. It is very important that we know the meaning of these words.

APPENDIX TWO: FUNDAMENTAL BAPTIST FELLOWSHIP INTERNATIONAL RESOLUTIONS ON TRANSLATIONS (pp. 359-362)

the KJV Is Not "Inspired"

STATEMENT #245. (p. 359) "Appendix Two" is entitled, *"Fundamental Baptist Fellowship International Resolutions on Translations."* the FBF is a group that is led, for the most part, by Bob Jones University graduates. On p. 361, Sproul wrote: *"Fundamentalists must exercise careful discernment in both the selection and rejection of translations. Some professing Fundamentals have wrongly declared one translation to be the only inspired copy of God's Word in the English language, and some make it a test of fundamentalism."*

COMMENT #245. First of all, I do not believe that the King James Bible is "*the only inspired copy of God's Word in the English language*." I do not believe there is any "*inspired*" translation in any language of the world. As I have mentioned often before, the original Hebrew, Aramaic, and Greek Words were the only Words that were "*given by inspiration of God,*" "*God-breathed,*" "*inspired of God,*" or "*inspired.*" Sproul once again charges all of us who use and defend the King James Bible with believing a false Ruckman view of that Bible. God did not "*breathe-out*" the King James Bible or any other translation in the world. It is the only accurate translation in the English language of the original, inspired, inerrant, infallible, preserved Hebrew, Aramaic, and Greek Words that underlie it.

I believe in the preservation of the Hebrew, Aramaic, and Greek Words underlying the King James Bible. Sproul, his Fundamental Baptist Fellowship,

Bob Jones University, Detroit Baptist Seminary, Central Baptist Seminary, Calvary Baptist Seminary, Northland Baptist College, Maranatha Baptist Bible College, International Baptist College, and many other Fundamentalist schools, pastors, and teachers do not believe this, sad to say.

APPENDIX THREE: BOOK REVIEW OF *"TOUCH NOT the UNCLEAN THING"* (pp. 363-372)

No "False Assertions"

STATEMENT #246. Appendix Number Three, Page 363, "Book Review of *Touch Not the Unclean Thing*" by Douglas Kutilek. *Touch Not the Unclean Thing* was written by Dr. David Sorenson who is at present one of our Dean Burgon Society Advisory Council members. Sproul says, on page 365, *"This book takes its cues from __false assertions__ of D. O. Fuller, D. A. Waite, and David Cloud, and therefore sadly disappoints."*

COMMENT #246. Kutilek does not give any of what he terms "*__false assertions__*" from these three men. It is his opinion that they exist, but he has not yet mentioned any of them. Each of the three men have written extensively in defense of the King James Bible and its underlying Hebrew, Aramaic, and Greek Words, which Kutilek has questioned in his many articles on the subject. He does not like any of the three of us. That is his privilege.

TR Is the "Traditional" Text

STATEMENT #247 (p. 365) Kutilek commented on David Sorenson's book, *Touch Not the Unclean Thing.* He wrote: *"He fails miserably and utterly to adequately __distinguish the term Textus Receptus (TR) from the terms Byzantine or traditional, ecclesiastical or majority Text__, treating the Textus Receptus as though it were the same meaning as these terms."*

COMMENT #247. Kutilek, and Sproul who quotes him, are both in error as far as being able to "*__distinguish the term Textus Receptus (TR) from the terms Byzantine or traditional, ecclesiastical or majority Text__.*" Dean John W. Burgon, in his book, *the Revision Revised*, p. 269 stated:

"The one great Fact, which especially troubles him and his joint Editor,

[speaking of Hort and Westcott here]--*(as well it may)--is the Traditional Greek Text of the New Testament Scriptures. Call this Text Erasmian or Complutensian--the Text of Stephens, or of Beza, or of the Elzevirs,--call it the "received" or the Traditional Greek Text or whatever other name you please;--the fact remains, that a Text has come down to us which is attested by a general consensus of ancient copies, ancient Fathers, ancient versions.*"

It is true that the so-called "*Majority Text*" is a more recent Text, the "*Received*" Text is one of the names Dean Burgon uses for the "Traditional Greek Text." He said you could "*call it . . . whatever other name you please.*" That would include the "*Byzantine*" or the "*ecclesiastical*" or the "*Majority Text.*" I agree with Burgon's combination of all of these various names.

STATEMENT #248. (p. 365) "The terms 'Byzantine' . . . or 'traditional' or 'ecclesiastical' as used by advocates of that Text, **including Burgon**, refer to the Text preserved in the majority of manuscripts, or, in short, a Text virtually identical to those published Greek texts of Hodges-Farstad and Robinson-Pierpont, **not the Erasmian texts collectively referred to as the Textus Receptus.**"

COMMENT #248. Kutilek and Sproul are misquoting Dean Burgon. In the above quote from *the Revision Revised*, (p. 369), Dean Burgon clearly includes "*received*" in the same group as the "*Traditional Greek Text.*" Dean Burgon felt that these two terms--"*or whatever other term you please*"--refer to "*a Text has come down to us which is attested by a general consensus of ancient copies, ancient Fathers, ancient versions.*" Neither Kutilek nor Sproul agree with this position. I do.

As to the "*received*" Text being also the "*majority*" Text, Dr. Jack Moorman has some information on this point. In his excellent book, *Forever Settled* (**BFT #1428 @ $20.00**), Dr. Moorman has identified the different manuscripts that Kurt Aland had in Munster, Germany as of 1967. He is now dead, and his wife Barbara, has taken over his work. In 1967 Kurt Aland had 5,255 Greek manuscripts of the New Testament. There have been 100 or 300 more since then. I would assume that the percentages would be similar.

Of these 5,255 Greek manuscripts, there were only the Vatican ("B"), the Sinai (Aleph) and 43 others for a total of 45 (less than 1%) that go along with the Critical Greek Text of Westcott and Hort, Nestle/Aland, and the United Bible Societies. The remaining 5,210 (over 99%) go along with the Words of the Traditional Received Text and the Words that underlie the King James Bible.

A Twisted "Textus Receptus" View

STATEMENT #249. (p. 366) Kutilek said, " *there is no such thing as the TR . . . the Textus Receptus,* [was] *a term first used in 1624,* [for printed texts] . . . *dating from 1514 to 1633 loosely called the Textus Receptus."*

COMMENT #249. When Kutilek stated that "*the Textus Receptus*" was a term was "*first used in 1624,*" seems to imply that the "*received Text*" began in 1624. This is a completely false assumption. This is a Text that has its origins from the Apostolic times.

"Infallible Transmission" Is True

STATEMENT #250. (p. 369) Kutilek said: *"Sorenson claims infallible transmission of the inspired Text. . . . This is an absolutely impossible position, and one which no one who has even a passing acquaintance with Greek manuscripts and printed editions would ever claim."*

COMMENT #250. Kutilek does not quote Sorenson, so I don't know if he said this or not. When the Lord Jesus Christ uttered these words: "*Heaven and earth shall pass away, but my words shall not pass away*" (Matthew 24:35) I believe He promised to insure the perfect preservation of these Words. Granted, each manuscript we have is not perfect, but the traditional texts taken as a whole allows us to discern the correct Words. This is because the traditional Text is so unified in its Words far more so than the Critical Text which is massively divergent. This is the reason I believe (though I cannot prove it to Kutilek, Sproul, or any other Critical Text people) the Hebrew, Aramaic, and Greek Words underlying the King James Bible are the original preserved Words of the "*inspired Text.*"

> Neither Kutilek nor Sproul are certain as to what Hebrew, Aramaic, or Greek Words have been preserved, or if any of them have been preserved. they are free to disbelieve, but I think it is a depressing situation for any Christian much less a Pastor to be in. I believe this is truly a lamentable position.

"Critical Text" Not "Orthodox Doctrine"

STATEMENT #251. (p. 171) Kutilek said: *"Sorenson closes . . . his book with an appeal for ecclesiastical separation by Fundamentalists from critical texts since they are tainted . . . by apostasy and unbelief. He fails utterly to show how a single variant reading accepted in the critical Text teaches anything other than orthodox doctrine."*

COMMENT #251. My friends, orthodox doctrine is questioned in 356 places where the "*critical Text* teaches" some things "*other than orthodox doctrine.*" These 356 places can be found on pages 119 to 312 of the 456-page hardback book by Dr. Jack Moorman. It is called *Early Manuscripts, Church Fathers, and the Authorized Version* (BFT #3230 @ $20.00 + $7.00 S&H). The reason for these false teachings is that the critical Text of Westcott and Hort, Nestle-Aland, and United Bible Societies is based on the

Gnostic-tainted manuscripts of the Vatican ("B") and Sinai (Aleph).

Here are just twenty of "<u>*other than orthodox doctrines*</u>" that are found in the critical Greek texts of our day:

● 1. In 1 Timothy 3:16, by removing the word, "*God,*" the critical Greek Text denies the "<u>*orthodox doctrine*</u>" of the incarnation of God the Son.

● 2. In 1 Corinthians 15:47, by removing the word, "*Lord,*" the critical Greek Text denies the "<u>*orthodox doctrine*</u>" of the deity of the Lord Jesus Christ.

● 3. In 1 John 4:3, by removing the words "*Christ is come in the flesh,*" the critical Greek Text denies the "<u>*orthodox doctrine*</u>" of the incarnation of the Lord Jesus Christ and that Jesus is also Christ.

● 4. In Matthew 1:25, by removing the word, "*firstborn,*" the critical Greek Text denies the "<u>*orthodox doctrine*</u>" of the virgin birth of the Lord Jesus Christ.

● 5. In Matthew 18:11, by removing the words, "*For the Son of man is come to save that which was lost,*" the critical Greek Text denies the "<u>*orthodox doctrine*</u>" of the significant mission of the Lord Jesus Christ to save the lost.

● 6. In Luke 9:56, by removing the words, "*For the Son of man is not come to destroy men's lives, but to save them,*" the critical Greek Text denies the "<u>*orthodox doctrine*</u>" of the significant mission of the Lord Jesus Christ to save the lost.

● 7. In Luke 2:22, by changing the word, "*her*" to "*their,*" the critical Greek Text denies the "<u>*orthodox doctrine*</u>" of the impeccability or sinlessness of the Lord Jesus Christ and contradicts the Old Testament procedure for "*purification*" procedure.

● 8. In John 7:8, by removing the first occurrence of "*yet,*" the critical Greek Text denies the "<u>*orthodox doctrine*</u>" of the truthfulness of the Lord Jesus Christ, thus making Him a liar.

● 9. In Ephesians 3:9, by removing the words, "*by Jesus Christ,*" the critical Greek Text denies the "<u>*orthodox doctrine*</u>" that the Lord Jesus Christ was, along with God the Father, the Creator.

● 10. In John 8:59, by removing the words, "*going through the midst of them and so passed by,*" the critical Greek Text denies the "<u>*orthodox doctrine*</u>" of the omnipotence of the Lord Jesus Christ.

● 11. In 2 Corinthians 4:14, by removing the word, "*by*" and replacing it with the word, "*with,*" the critical Greek Text denies the "<u>*orthodox doctrine*</u>" of the power of the Lord Jesus Christ to raise the dead and also the fact of His bodily

● 12. In 1 Corinthians 5:7, by removing the words, "*for us,*" the critical Greek Text denies the "*orthodox doctrine*" of the vicarious, substitutionary sacrifice of the Lord Jesus Christ.

● 13. In Galatians 4:7, by removing the words, "*through Christ,*" the critical Greek Text denies the "*orthodox doctrine*" of salvation and sonship only through the Lord Jesus Christ

● 14. In Hebrews 1:3, by removing the words, "*by Himself,*" the critical Greek Text denies the "*orthodox doctrine*" of salvation only through the Lord Jesus Christ without anyone else or anything else "*purging our sins.*"

● 15. In John 3:15, by removing the words, "*should not perish,*" the critical Greek Text denies the "*orthodox doctrine*" of the perishing in Hell for those who do not believe on the Lord Jesus Christ for salvation.

● 16. In 2 Peter 2:17, by removing the words, "*for ever,*" the critical Greek Text denies the "*orthodox doctrine*" the "*darkness*" of Hell is everlasting for those who do not receive the Lord Jesus Christ as the ir Saviour.

● 17. In John 6:47, by removing the words, "*on me,*" the critical Greek Text denies the "*orthodox doctrine*" of believing on the Lord Jesus Christ as being essential for "*everlasting life.*"

● 18. In Romans 1:16, by removing the words, "*of Christ,*" the critical Greek Text denies the "*orthodox doctrine*" of the necessity of including "*Christ*" in the Bible's only "*gospel*" and only way of "*salvation.*"

● 19. In John 6:47, by removing the words, "*on me,*" the critical Greek Text denies the "*orthodox doctrine*" of believing on the Lord Jesus Christ as being essential for "*everlasting life.*"

● 20. In Philippians 4:13, by removing the word, "*Christ,*" the critical Greek Text denies the "*orthodox doctrine*" that only the Lord Jesus Christ can strengthen the believing Christians.

For a listing 158 of the more significant doctrinal passages from the 356 doctrinal passages uncovered by Dr. Jack Moorman, you can read about them in Chapter V of my book, *Defending the King James Bible* (BFT #1594 @ $12.00 + $4.00 S&H).

APPENDIX FOUR: BOOK REVIEW OF "*THOU SHALT KEEP THEM*" (pp. 373-394)

Denying "Preservation of the Text"

STATEMENT #252. (p. 375) Appendix #4 is a book review by Keith Gephart of the book, *Thou Shalt Keep them* written by Kent Brandenburg. Gephart is a professor of International Baptist College of Tempe, Arizona, Sproul's school. Gephart wrote: "*However, it is sad that the y will not fellowship with those fundamentalists who hold to either the majority Text or critical Text positions--even though <u>those fundamentalists fervently believe in and fight for the verbal, plenary inspiration and inerrancy of Scripture</u>; They clearly call for separation from any who do not hold to <u>their particular position on the preservation of the Text.</u>*"

     COMMENT #252. It is a blatant falsehood for Gephart to say that "<u>*those fundamentalists fervently believe in and fight for the verbal, plenary inspiration and inerrancy of Scripture.*</u>" This statement implies that these "<u>*majority Text*</u>" and "<u>*critical Text*</u>" people "<u>*fervently believe in and fight for*</u>" the "<u>*inerrancy of Scripture.*</u>" The "<u>*Scripture*</u>" implied is the Hebrew, Aramaic, and Greek Words of the originals. This is what they do **NOT** "<u>*believe in and fight for.*</u>" In fact, the y "<u>*fight*</u>" **against** the book's "<u>*position on the preservation of the Text*</u>" which is true "<u>*inerrancy.*</u>" Gephart is up to the same re-definition of terms as Sproul and his anti-traditional Text Fundamentalist friends.

  Plenary verbal "<u>*preservation*</u>" of the original Hebrew, Aramaic, and Greek Words is of vital importance. Gephart, Sproul, and their Fundamentalist friends despise that true "<u>*inerrancy*</u>" position. I do not want to have close fellowship with those people who are denying that true Biblical position.

Don't Trust "Textual Criticism"

STATEMENT #253. (p. 376) Gephart says, *"The Textus Receptus originated through __textual criticism__. All the editions of the TR and all the translations of it, including the KJV, are the result of textual criticism."*

COMMENT #253. Nowhere does Gephart define what he means by "*__textual criticism__*." The slipshod and lying methods used today under the name of "*__textual criticism__*" were not used either for the "*__Textus Receptus__*" or for the "*__KJV__*." The "*__Textus Receptus__*" was the result of the agreement of thousands of Greek Manuscripts. There was not "*family*" or "*genealogical*" false hypotheses used by Bishop Westcott, Professor Hort and the ir modern followers. Scores of other phony practices used by modern day "*__textual criticism__*" were never used either for the "*__Textus Receptus__*" or for the "*__KJV__*." The implications here are totally false and misleading.

Verbal "Preservation" Is Essential

STATEMENT #254. (p. 377) Gephart quotes *Thou Shalt Keep Them's* definition of "*__preservation__*" as the "*__thesis of the book__*." Here is the quote: "*__Complete, inerrant protection__ and general accessibility of every writing (vowels and consonants, words, and order of letters and words) of the Bible, the 66 books of the Old and New Testaments for every generation of believers.*"

COMMON #254. Gephart can't stand this definition of "*preservation*" as "*__Complete, inerrant protection__*." And yet he wrote previously that he (and other anti-Textus Receptus men) "*__fervently believed in and fought for__*" what he called "*__inerrancy of Scripture__*." the above definition is true "inerrancy of Scripture" which is totally denied by Gephart, Sproul, and his Fundamentalist followers.

The "Received Text" in 2nd Century

STATEMENT #255. (p. 377) "*. . . there was __no 'Received Text in the second century__ in the sense as defined by these authors and present in the Text of Scrivener.*"

COMMENT #255. How does Gephart know this? Was he there in the "*__second century__*"? Of course he wasn't. This was the century immediately following the origination of the New Testament. It was a century where the originals themselves were present. The heresy that Gephart is promulgating here is the falsehood that the "Received Text" was not the Apostolic Text, but that it was not in existence until 500 or 600 A.D. or later. The reason for this heresy is that Gephart has swallowed the false secularistic brand of "*__textual criticism__*."

> There was a "*__Received Text__*" in the "*__second century__*." There has been

a "_Received Text_" ever since the apostles lived. Paul, Peter, James, John, Jude, Matthew, Mark, Luke and the rest of them had the "_Received Text_" from the first century and onward. It was the Text of the original Greek manuscripts.

"Preservation" Helps the "Godly"

STATEMENT #256. (p. 379) "_A promise of the preservation of God's literal words in some written form would not help the **godly** if **the truth of the words** was not actually applied to them._"

            COMMENT #256. The "_truth of the words_" have been applied to the "_godly_." They have been applied to those who are Christians. These Words have done some good because God has preserved His Hebrew, Aramaic, and Greek Words to this day for the "_godly_."

"Matthew 4:4" Defends "Preservation"

STATEMENT #257. (p. 380) Gephart says, "_Mat the w 4:4 does not make the promise_ that God would see to it that _man would have every word_ available to him despite his sinful disobedience and neglect._"

            COMMENT #257. Since Gephart said that "_Matthew 4:4 does not make the promise_," let's see what Matthew 4:4 says. The Lord Jesus Christ is answering the Devil:
    "_But he answered and said, It is written, Man shall not live by bread alone, but by **every word that proceedeth out of the mouth of God**._"
How can a person "_live_" by "_every word that proceedeth out of the mouth of God_" if he does not have "_every word that proceedeth out of the mouth of God_"? This is a definite promise by the Lord Jesus Christ Himself of the preservation of the original Hebrew, Aramaic, and Greek Words of the Bible.

"It Is Written" For "Preservation"

STATEMENT #258. (p. 380) "_Strouse uses the expression, 'It is written' to show the 'verbal, plenary preservation of God's Words' (p. 39). The statement cannot be so pressed into the service of Strouse's theory. True, God has preserved the verse quoted (which **does not at all apply to the doctrine of preservation**) or it could not be quoted here. But '**it is written' is not a statement of preservation**, . . ._"

            COMMENT #258. Gephart's statement is absolutely false. The expression in Matthew 4:4, "_It is written_," is the word GEGRAPTAI. This Greek word is used 67 times in the Greek New Testament. That is a Greek perfect tense from the verb GRAPHO which means "_to write_."

Gephart's denial of preservation by the use of this perfect tense is erroneous. If he would get out *A Manual Grammar of the Greek New Testament* by Dana and Mantey and turn to paragraph 182 on page 200 (or some other competent Greek grammar book), he would find out about the significance of the Greek perfect tense.

> "*It implies a process, but views that process as having reached its consummation and existing in a finished state.*" [Dana and Mantey, *A Manual Grammar of the Greek New Testament*, para. 182, p. 200]

It has been established that the perfect tense views an action as having been completed in the past, and having the results continuing as a "*finished state*" into the present and future. GEGRAPTAI speaks of the Words of God which were written inerrantly in the past, and continue in an inerrant state into the present and future. This is, by very definition, the Bible's definition of the doctrine of plenary, verbal preservation of the original Hebrew, Aramaic, and Greek Words of the Bible.

Matthew 5:17-18 For Preservation

STATEMENT #259. (p. 381) He is talking about Matthew 5:17-18 and Gephart says, "*Despite the argument of Gary Webb to the contrary, this passage does not discuss the preservation of the physical Text of the Scriptures.*"

COMMENT #259. When talking about Matthew 5:18, Gephart is in total error when he says: "*this passage does not discuss the preservation of the physical Text of the Scriptures.*" Take a look at this verse below:

> "*For verily I say unto you, Till Heaven and earth pass, one jot or one tittle shall in no wise pass from the law, till all be fulfilled.*" (Matthew 5:18)

The Lord Jesus Christ is very clear that "*Till Heaven and earth pass,*" There will be a "**preservation**" of even the smallest letter and the smallest vowel of the Hebrew language. The "*jot*" or "*Yodh*" is the smallest Hebrew letter. It is like our "*comma,*" single quotation mark, or an "*apostrophe.*" The "*tittle*" or "*Chireq*" is the smallest Hebrew vowel point. It is like our "*period.*" This verse is referring to the written Words of God being preserved down to the smallest letter and part of a letter. Gephart is, in effect, calling the Lord Jesus Christ a liar when He promised that the smallest Hebrew letters and parts of letters would be preserved.

A Tittle" Is A "Vowel Point"

STATEMENT #260. (p. 381) "*Gary Webb states on page 44 that the tittle includes the vowel points. That argument is absolutely false and is based solely on human reason--not divine revelation.*"

COMMENT #260. Gephart is in total error once again about the "_tittle_." It is a "_dot_," and the only single "_dot_" in Hebrew language is the "_chireq_." Where did Gephart get his false information on what the "_tittle_" is?   Here are some of the definitions of "_tittle_."

●1. According to the Wikipedia entry, a "_tittle_" is defined as follows:

   "_A tittle is a small distinguishing mark, such as a diacritic or the dot on a lowercase i or j. The tittle is an integral part of the glyph of i and j, but diacritic dots can appear over other letters in various languages._"

●2. According to the _Dictionary.com Unabridged (v 1.1)_ Based on the Random House _Unabridged Dictionary_, 2006, a "_tittle_" is defined as follows:

   1. a dot or other small mark in writing or printing, used as a diacritic, punctuation, etc.

●3. According to the _Merriam-Webster online search dictionary_, a "_tittle_" is defined as follows:

   1. a point or small sign used as a diacritical mark in writing or printing

●4. According to _the Free Dictionary_ a "_tittle_" is defined as follows:

   1. _A small diacritic mark, such as an accent, vowel mark, or dot over an i._

As I mentioned in the previous **STATEMENT #256**, the "_tittle_" in the Hebrew language is the smallest vowel, called the "_chireq_" or simple "_dot_."

Matthew 28:30 For "Preservation"

STATEMENT #261. (p. 383) Remarking on Matthew 28:30 Gephart said: "_Christ instructed his disciples to teach new believers' to observe all things whatsoever I have commanded you.' The command is obedience to Christ's commands; the verse does not describe a written preservation of the Text of the commands._"

   COMMENT #261. How can Gephart, with a straight face, state that "_the verse does not describe a written preservation of the Text_"? If the Lord Jesus wants us "_to observe all things whatsoever He has commanded us_," how can we possibly do this unless His "_commands_" are preserved for us? The answer to both of these questions, for everyone except Gephart, is a no-brainer.

Matthew 24:35 For "Preservation"

STATEMENT #262. (p. 384) When commenting on Matthew 24:35, Gephart said: "_Jesus does not say here that these words would all be put in writing and kept available in written form for every generation._"

COMMENT #262. One of the greatest no-brainers yet is Gephart's gross misinterpretation of Matthew 24:35. This is a verse which gives the Words of the Lord Jesus Christ Himself guaranteeing plenary, verbal preservation of every Word of the Hebrew, Aramaic Old Testament and Greek New Testament. It is repeated exactly in Mark 13:31 and Luke 21:33. Here are what these verses say:

"*Heaven and earth shall pass away, but my words shall not pass away.*"

If these Words do not teach that the Lord Jesus Christ promised us plenary, verbal preservation of all of His "Words," what do they promise? The Greek Word for "*not*" is OU ME which is the strongest negative in the Greek language. It means "*never, never, never.*"

The following verses show that the Lord Jesus Christ is the Author all of the New Testament Greek Words:

"*I have yet many things to say unto you, but ye cannot bear them now.* [13] *Howbeit when he, the Spirit of truth, is come, he will guide you into all truth: for he shall not speak of himself; but whatsoever he shall hear, that shall he speak: and he will shew you things to come.* [14] *He shall glorify me: for he shall receive of mine, and shall shew it unto you.*" (John 16:12-14)

By extension, as the Word and Revelator, He is also the Author of all of the Hebrew and Aramaic Words of the Old Testament. In view of this, He has promised plenary, verbal original Bible preservation, despite Gephart's denial of this promise.

"Words" Not "Word" Only

STATEMENT #263. (p. 385) "*Genuine fundamentalists do not disagree with the teaching on the preservation of God's Word and words. His Word does abide forever is able to and does save sinners until the end the end of the age.*"

COMMENT #263. You'll notice that Gephart talked about "*the preservation of God's Word and words.*" He should have stopped the phrase with "*the preservation of God's Word*" because neither he nor Sproul, nor their fellow critical Text Fundamentalist friends believe in the "*preservation of God's . . . words.*" They believe only in "*the preservation of God's Word,*" by which they mean only the "*ideas, thoughts, concepts, message, truth, or teachings*" have been "*preserved,*" but not the "*Words.*" This is sheer hypocrisy and is false at its very base. If you want to see quotation after quotation from various so-called "*Genuine fundamentalists*" that deny the "*preservation*" of the "*Words,*" but only their re-defined (as above) "*Word*" of God, see some of my books.

> ● **1.** *Fundamentalist Deception on Bible Preservation* (BFT #3234 @ $8.00 + $4.00 S&H).
>
> ● **2.** *Bob Jones University's ERRORS on Bible Preservation* (BFT #3259 @ $8.00 + $4.00 S&H).
>
> ● **3.** *Fundamentalist Mis-Information on Bible Versions* (BFT #2974 @ $7.00 + $4.00 S&H).

This false and unscriptural position is held in the books, speeches, and writings of faculty members made by or published by such Fundamentalist groups as Bob Jones University, Central Baptist Seminary, Detroit Baptist Seminary, Calvary Baptist Seminary, Northland Baptist College, and others.

STATEMENT #264. (p. 386) Gephart comments on the words, "*It is Written.*" He wrote: "*However, Sutton portrays a basic misunderstanding of the nature of the perfect tense in his use of the expression. It is not true that the perfect tense states that 'in the verse at hand was written in the past and the results continue to be written down.*'"

COMMENT #264. Let me repeat what I have stated in **COMMENT #255:**

Gephart's denial of preservation by the use of this perfect tense is erroneous. If he would get out a *Manual Grammar of the Greek New Testament* by Dana and Mantey and turn to paragraph 182 on page 200 (or some other competent Greek grammar book), he would find out about the significance of the Greek perfect tense.

"*It implies a process, but views that process as having reached its consummation and existing in a finished state.*" [Dana and Mantey, *A Manual Grammar of the Greek New Testament*, para. 182, p. 200]

> It has been established that the perfect tense views an action as having been completed in the past, and having the results continuing as a "*finished state*" into the present and future. GEGRAPTAI speaks of the Words of God which were written inerrantly in the past, and continue in an inerrant state into the present and future. This is, by very definition, the Bible's definition of the doctrine of plenary, verbal preservation of the original Hebrew, Aramaic, and Greek Words of the Bible.

The Meaning of "*It Is Written*"

STATEMENT #265. (p. 387) "*The Words, it is written, cannot prove that the actual words continue to exist. . . .*"

COMMENT #265. I have answered Gephart's false statement on the use of the Greek perfect tense in both **COMMENTS #255 and #261** above.

Three "Perverted" Bible Versions

STATEMENT #266. (p. 390) Gephart speaks about Dr. Thomas Corkish: *"He calls the NASV, the NIV, and NKJV 'perverted Bibles'* which take 'liberties in *changing the Words of God that God has breathed.' (p. 146). Again, such a statement is distorted, inaccurate and unchristian."*

 COMMENT #266. I also call "*the NASV, the NIV, and NKJV 'perverted Bibles."* The "*NASV and the NIV*" are "*perverted Bibles*" because the y have "*perverted*" the Hebrew, Aramaic, and Greek Words that underlie them.   By using perverted underlying original Words, these two translations are definitely guilty of "*changing the Words of God that God has breathed.*"

> In the English translations of those "*perverted*" Words "*that God has breathed*" out, they have "*perverted*" their translations as follows:
>
> 1.   The *NKJV* has translational additions, subtractions, or changes in some other way in over 2,000 places as I have documented in BFT #1442 @ $10.00 + $5.00 S&H.
>
> 2.   The *NASV* has translational additions, subtractions, or changes in some other way in over 4,000 places as I have documented in BFT #1494 @ $15.00 + $5.00 S&H.
>
> 3.   The *NIV* has translational additions, subtractions, or changes in some other way in over 6,653 places as I have documented in BFT #1749-P @ $25.00 + $5.00 S&H.

These "*perversions*" of the Words of God should be pointed out for every one in the world to see clearly.

"Verbal, Plenary Preservation"

STATEMENT #267. (p. 390)   Gephart commented on Kent Brandenburg's statement on page 203 of his book: *"'In the surviving manuscripts from the region of the Byzantine Empire . . . evidence essentially 98% agreement on the Words.' This is an admission there has not been 'verbal, plenary preservation.'"*

 COMMENT #267. Gephart fails to understand what happens when upwards of 98% (Dr. Jack Moorman found 99%) of the surviving 5,255 manuscripts (that Kurt Aland had in 1967) are in agreement with one another. When they are compared, it is relatively easy to find which Words are the product of "*verbal, plenary preservation.*"

"Perfect Preservation" Not "Aberrant"

STATEMENT #268. (p. 391)   Speaking of Dr. Thomas Corkish, Gephart wrote: *"He equates the Critical and Majority Text positions with 'profane* *and vain babblings' that will 'overthrow the faith of some (II Timothy 2:16, 19, 22; p. 218).' On the contrary, Dr. Mike Sproul's book shows conclusively that the position of the 'perfect preservation' is the aberrant view in the history of fundamentalism."*

COMMENT #268. Well, if indeed, "*'perfect preservation' is the aberrant view in the history of fundamentalism*," then I would say that "*fundamentalism*" is wrong in this area of the Bible. "*Fundamentalism*" has been wrong in other areas, so why count it as inerrant and infallible as Gephart and Sproul have both been doing in this book? If indeed "*perfect preservation*" of the original Hebrew, Aramaic, and Greek Words is Biblical (and I believe that it is), why should people care what the "*history of fundamentalism*" thought about it?

"KJV" Is "Accurate," Not "Perfect"

STATEMENT #269. (p. 392) *"The majority of English speaking churches, both fundamental and evangelical, do not recognize the Text behind the KJV as a perfect Text. The wisdom of other language groups has kept them from making similar claims to textual perfections."*

COMMENT #269. I would probably have to agree with Gephart on this point that the "*majority of English speaking churches . . . do not recognize the Text behind the KJV as a perfect Text.*" Our Bible For Today ministry and our Dean Burgon Society ministry have a lot of educational work to do to convince this "*majority*" of the truth about this subject. This is an Article of Faith by both of the above groups.

Once again, the Words of the Lord Jesus Christ must be believed. The Lord Jesus Christ said: *"Heaven and earth shall pass away, but my Words shall not pass away"* (Matthew 24:35; Mark 13:31; and Luke 21:33). The Greek term for *"not"* is OU ME. This is the strongest Greek negative particle in the language. It means *"never, never."* This is an unmistakable promise of the *"preservation"* of the Bible's Hebrew, Aramaic, and Greek Words. I believe the Scriptures and the Lord Jesus Christ's promises.

Ignorance of the "Textus Receptus"

STATEMENT #270. (p. 392) Gephart wrote: *"LaMore's following statement is a blatant perversion of history: 'Only the Textus Receptus was preserved by God through His churches and available to every generation. (p. 234)' The Textus Receptus did not exist until the 16th Century. No evidence exists of a Text 'exactly' as Erasmus' till the 16th Century."*

COMMENT #270. I am sorry to say that Gephart is woefully ignorant of this subject and therefore should not be making such pontifical pronouncements. There are three major errors in his statement that "*the Textus*

Receptus did not exist until the 16th Century."

●**Error #1** is Gephart's apparent mistake when he said "*the 16th Century*." I believe he is referring to Elzevir's 1633 edition of the Greek New Testament where he first used the Latin term "*textum receptum*" in his preface. He said that it was a Text "*received by all*." If this is what was referred to, that would make it the **17th** Century rather than the *16th Century*.

●**Error #2** is Gephart's underlying and false belief that just because Elzevir used the term "*textum receptum*" in 1633 that is different from the "*Traditional or Received Text*" that had been "*received by all*" from Apostolic times. In actuality, in 1633, these two terms referred to the same thing.

●**Error #3** is Gephart's false belief that the "*Textus Receptus*," or "*received Text*," or "*traditional Text*" "*did not exist until the 16th Century*" or the 17th Century. The traditional Text was in the hands of early Church Fathers who died in 400 A.D. or before. Dean Burgon's book, *the Traditional Text*, on pages 99-100, outlines some research that he and his staff did regarding seventy-six early Church Fathers who died in 400 A.D. or before. He found that the traditional Text was found to be quoted or alluded to as opposed to the Critical (or "*neologian*", as he called it) Text in a ratio of 3 to 2 which would be 60% versus 40%. Dr. Jack Moorman made a similar research of over eighty early Church Fathers who died before 400 A.D. He found the traditional Text was quoted or alluded to as opposed to the critical Text in a ratio of 70% versus 30%. This certainly is substantial proof that the traditional, or received or Textus Receptus kind of Text was in existence well before 400 A.D. rather than believing that it "*did not exist until the 16th Century*."

"Preservation" a "Fundamental Truth"

STATEMENT #271. (p. 392) *"In Addendum B Thomas Strouse calls his view of preservation 'a fundament truth,' and those who do not hold to 'perfect preservation can hardly be called fundamentalist.'"*

COMMENT #271.   Though Gephart despises this statement, I agree with the statement. The "*perfect preservation*" of the Hebrew, Aramaic, and Greek Words underlying the King James Bible is truly "*a fundamental truth*" and those who call themselves "*fundamentalist*" do not deserve that title in this area of Bibliology though they might deserve it other areas of their theology.

This is the present position at Bob Jones University, Detroit Baptist Seminary, Central Baptist Seminary, Calvary Baptist Seminary, Northland Baptist College, Maranatha Baptist College in Wisconsin, and some other so-called "*fundamentalist*" schools. I've always taken the view that you can call them "*fundamentalist*" in some areas like the Virgin Birth of Christ but not in Bibliology. Dr. Strouse doesn't believe that you can call them "*fundamentalist*" at all because they do not believe in "*perfect preservation*." He may be right.

Time will tell.

God Promised Preservation

STATEMENT #272. (p. 393) *"BUT THAT IS NOT the ISSUE. GOD DID NOT SAY HE WOULD DO WHAT BRANDENBURG MAKES AN OBJECT OF FAITH."*

COMMENT #272. Gephart is in error as in many other places when he wrote *"GOD DID NOT SAY HE WOULD DO"* what Brandenburg said. Brandenburg believed that God said He would preserve His Hebrew, Aramaic, and Greek Words. Let me quote once again what the Lord Jesus Christ said in the same words in three different places in three of the four Gospels (Matthew 24:35; Mark 13:31; and Luke 21:33): *"Heaven and earth shall pass away, but My words shall not pass away."* That's a promise from the Lord Jesus Christ.

The Lord Jesus Christ also promised that *"one jot or one tittle shall in no wise pass from the law, till all be fulfilled"* (Matthew 5:18) has not been fulfilled. The *"jot"* or *"Yodh"* is the smallest Hebrew letter. It is like our *"comma,"* single quotation mark, or an *"apostrophe."* The *"tittle"* or *"Chireq"* is the smallest Hebrew vowel point. It is like our *"period."* Gephart is dead wrong in his assessment here. God did promise to preserve His Hebrew, Aramaic, and Greek Words.

A Lie About "Preservation"

STATEMENT #273. (p. 394) *"What all fundamentalists believe is in inspiration, inerrancy, infallibility and preservation; what fundamentalists disagree on is the interpretation of passages that may or may not indicate the method, means and location of God's preservation."*

COMMENT #273. Gephart is not correct in what he says *"all fundamentalists believe"* about *"God's preservation"* of His Hebrew, Aramaic, and Greek Words. The new double-speak redefinition of *"preservation"* by the so-called *"fundamentalists"* does not concern the *"Words"* of Hebrew, Aramaic, and Greek originals. In many of their recent books (which I have answered in many books of my own), these new-fangled *"fundamentalists"* completely redefine *"inspiration"* and remove it from the original Words of the Bible. They clearly state that they believe in only the *"preservation"* of the *"word"* of God which means to them only the *"ideas, thoughts, concepts, message, truth, or teachings"* of the Bible, but not the original *Words*.

The *"fundamentalist"* schools I refer to are Bob Jones University, Detroit Baptist Seminary, Central Baptist Seminary, Calvary Baptist Seminary, Northland Baptist College, Maranatha Baptist College in Wisconsin, and some other so-called *"fundamentalist"* schools.

God's Perfect "Words" Preservation

STATEMENT #274. (p. 394) *"The only view based on a response of faith in God's Word is the view that God has perfectly preserved His Words and that they are and have been available to every generation."*

COMMENT #274. This, of course, Gephart does not agree with this statement, but I do. This is exactly what God has done for us.

APPENDIX FIVE: BOOK REVIEW OF *"WHICH TEXT?"* (pp. 395-400)

Criticism of Matthew Not Burgon's

STATEMENT #275. (p. 395, 399) Appendix Five is a "Book Review of *'Which Text.'"* The reviewer is Sproul himself. The author of the book is Charles Surrett who is a teacher at Ambassador Baptist College. Referring to Surrett, Sproul wrote: *"He sites and refers to men like Burgon who was a nineteenth century Majority Text opponent of Westcott and Hort, in a most favorable manner. Yet, Surrett never informs the reader that <u>when Burgon actually did the textual criticism on the book of Matthew</u>, that the Text he created was very similar to a modern Majority Text and dissimilar to the TR when there are variants."*

COMMENT #275. This quotation by Sproul is one more indication of his inaccurate knowledge in these matters of the Bible's Text. Sproul wrote about a time "<u>when Burgon actually did the textual criticism on the book of Matthew</u>." There are several errors in this statement:

- ●1. "*<u>Burgon</u>*" never did any "<u>*textual criticism on the book of Matthew*</u>." the book Sproul refers to is *A Textual Commentary upon the Holy Gospels Part I. ST. MATTHEW; Division 1. i-xiv.* This book is limited to Matthew 1-14, rather than the entire book.
- ●2. Though Miller uses Burgon's name in the book, the author of this book is not "*<u>Burgon</u>*" but "*Edward Miller, M.A. Bursalis Prebendary in the Cathedral of Chichester.*"
- ●3. The book was published in London by George Bell & Sons, Cambridge: Deighton Bell & Co. The date of publication was <u>**1899**</u>. Dean John William Burgon lived from <u>**1813 to 1888.**</u> Burgon had been dead 11 years when this book was published, making it impossible for him to be its author.

APPENDIX SIX:
DOES KJV-ONLYISM EXTEND
BACK TO FREDRICK NOLAN
IN A.D. 1815?
(pp. 401-405)

There are no questions or comments made on this APPENDIX SIX. It is listed here by title in order to be complete.

Index of Words and Phrases

About the Author

The author of this book, Dr. D. A. Waite, received a B.A. (Bachelor of Arts) in classical Greek and Latin from the University of Michigan in 1948, a Th.M. (Master of Theology), with high honors, in New Testament Greek Literature and Exegesis from Dallas Theological Seminary in 1952, an M.A. (Master of Arts) in Speech from Southern Methodist University in 1953, a Th.D. (Doctor of Theology), with honors, in Bible Exposition from Dallas Theological Seminary in 1955, and a Ph.D. in Speech from Purdue University in 1961. He holds both New Jersey and Pennsylvania teacher certificates in Greek and Language Arts.

He has been a teacher in the areas of Greek, Hebrew, Bible, Speech, and English for over thirty-five years in ten schools, including one junior high, one senior high, three Bible institutes, two colleges, two universities, and one seminary. He served his country as a Navy Chaplain for five years on active duty; pastored two churches; was Chairman and Director of the Radio and Audio-Film Commission of the American Council of Christian Churches; since 1971, has been Founder, President, and Director of THE BIBLE FOR TODAY; since 1978, has been President of the DEAN BURGON SOCIETY; has produced over 700 other studies, books, cassettes, or VCR's on various topics; and is heard on both a five-minute daily and thirty-minute weekly radio program IN DEFENSE OF TRADITIONAL BIBLE TEXTS, on radio, and streaming on the Internet at www.BibleForToday.org, 24/7/365. Dr. and Mrs. Waite have been married since 1948; they have four sons, one daughter, and, at present, eight grandchildren, and five great-grandchildren. Since October 4, 1998, he has been the Pastor of The Bible For Today Baptist Church in Collngswood, New Jersey. The Church Phone is: 856-854-4747.

Order Blank (p. 1)

Name:_____

Address:_____

City & State:_____Zip:_____

Credit Card #:_____Expires:_____

The Most Recently Published Books

[ ] Send *A Critical Answer to God's Word Preserved* by Dr. D. A. Waite, 184 pp. perfect bound ($11.00+$4.00 S&H)

[ ] Send *BJU's Errors on Bible Preservation* by Dr. D. A. Waite, 120 pages, paperback ($8+$4 S&H) fully indexed

[ ] Send *Romans—Preaching Verse by Verse* by Pastor D. A. Waite 736 pp. Hardback ($25+$5 S&H) fully indexed

[ ] *Early Manuscripts, Church Fathers, & the Authorized Version* by Dr. Jack Moorman, $18+$5 S&H. Hardback

[ ] Send *The LIE That Changed the Modern World* by Dr. H. D. Williams ($16+$5 S&H) Hardback book

[ ] Send *With Tears in My Heart* by Gertrude G. Sanborn. Hardback 414 pp. ($25+$5 S&H) 400 Christian Poems

Preaching Verse by Verse Books

[ ] Send *Romans—Preaching Verse by Verse* by Pastor D. A. Waite 736 pp. Hardback ($25+$5 S&H) fully indexed

[ ] Send *Colossians & Philemon—Preaching Verse by Verse* by Pastor D. A. Waite ($12+$5 S&H) hardback, 240 pages.

[ ] Send *Philippians—Preaching Verse by Verse* by Pastor D. A. Waite ($10+$5 S&H) hardback, 176 pages.

[ ] Send *Ephesians—Preaching Verse by Verse* by Pastor D. A. Waite ($12+$5 S&H) hardback, 224 pages.

[ ] Send *Galatians—Preaching Verse By Verse* by Pastor D. A. Waite ($12+$5 S&H) hardback, 216 pages.

[ ] Send *First Peter—Preaching Verse By Verse* by Pastor D. A. Waite ($10+$5 S&H) hardback, 176 pages.

Send or Call Orders to:
THE BIBLE FOR TODAY
900 Park Ave., Collingswood, NJ 08108
Phone: 856-854-4452; FAX:--2464; Orders: 1-800 JOHN 10:9

Order Blank (p. 2)

Name:_____

Address:_____

City & State:_____Zip:_____

Credit Card #:_____Expires:_____

Books on Bible Texts & Translations

[ ] Send *Defending the King James Bible* by Dr. Waite ($12+$5 S&H) A hardback book, indexed with study questions.

[ ] Send *BJU's Errors on Bible Preservation* by Dr. D. A. Waite, 110 pages, paperback ($8+$4 S&H) fully indexed

[ ] Send *Fundamentalist Deception on Bible Preservation* by Dr.Waite, ($8+$4 S&H), paperback, fully indexed

[ ] Send *Fundamentalist MIS-INFORMATION on Bible Versions* by Dr. Waite ($7+$4 S&H) perfect bound, 136 pages

[ ] Send *Fundamentalist Distortions on Bible Versions* by Dr. Waite ($6+$3 S&H) A perfect bound book, 80 pages

[ ] Send *Fuzzy Facts From Fundamentalists* by Dr. D. A. Waite ($8.00 + $4.00) printed booklet

[ ] Send *Foes of the King James Bible Refuted* by DAW ($10 +$4 S&H) A perfect bound book, 164 pages in length.

[ ] Send *Central Seminary Refuted on Bible Versions* by Dr. Waite ($10+$4 S&H) A perfect bound book, 184 pages

[ ] Send *The Case for the King James Bible* by DAW ($7 +$3 S&H) A perfect bound book, 112 pages in length.

[ ] Send *Theological Heresies of Westcott and Hort* by Dr. D. A. Waite, ($7+$3 S&H) A printed booklet.

[ ] Send *Westcott's Denial of Resurrection*, Dr. Waite ($4+$3)

[ ] Send *Four Reasons for Defending KJB* by DAW ($3+$3)

Send or Call Orders to:
THE BIBLE FOR TODAY
900 Park Ave., Collingswood, NJ 08108
Phone: 856-854-4452; FAX:--2464; Orders: 1-800

Order Blank (p. 3)

Name:_____

Address:_____

City & State:_____Zip:_____

Credit Card #:_____Expires:_____

More Books on Texts & Translations

[ ] Send *Holes in the Holman Christian Standard Bible* by Dr.
Waite ($3+$2 S&H) A printed booklet, 40 pages
[ ] Send *Contemporary Eng. Version Exposed*, DAW ($3+$2)
[ ] Send *NIV Inclusive Language Exposed* by DAW ($5+$3)
[ ] Send *26 Hours of KJB Seminar* (4 videos) by DAW ($50.00)

Books By Dr. Jack Moorman

[ ] *Early Manuscripts, Church Fathers, & the Authorized
Version* by Dr. Jack Moorman, $18+$5 S&H. Hardback
[ ] Send *Forever Settled—Bible Documents & History Survey*
by Dr. Jack Moorman, $20+$5 S&H. Hardback book.
[ ] Send *When the KJB Departs from the So-Called "Majority
Text"* by Dr. Jack Moorman, $16+$5 S&H
[ ] Send *Missing in Modern Bibles—Nestle-Aland & NIV Errors*
by Dr. Jack Moorman, $8+$4 S&H
[ ] Send *The Doctrinal Heart of the Bible—Removed from Mod-
ern Versions* by Dr. Jack Moorman, VCR, $15 +$4 S&H
[ ] Send *Modern Bibles—The Dark Secret* by Dr. Jack Moor-
man, $5+$3 S&H
[ ] Send *Samuel P. Tregelles—The Man Who Made the Critical
Text Acceptable to Bible Believers* by Dr. Moorman ($2+$1)
[ ] Send *8,000 Differences Between TR & CT* by Dr. Jack
Moorman [$65 + $7.50 S&H] Over 500-large-pages of data
[ ] Send *356 Doctrinal Errors in the NIV & Other Modern
Versions*, 100-large-pages, $10.00+$6 S&H.

Send or Call Orders to:
THE BIBLE FOR TODAY
900 Park Ave., Collingswood, NJ 08108
Phone: 856-854-4452; FAX:--2464; Orders: 1-800

Order Blank (p. 4)

Name:_____

Address:_____

City & State:_____Zip:_____

Credit Card #:_____Expires:_____

Books By or About Dean Burgon

[ ] Send *The Revision Revised* by Dean Burgon ($25 + $5
S&H) A hardback book, 640 pages in length.

[ ] Send *The Last 12 verses of Mark* by Dean Burgon ($15+$5
S&H) A hardback book 400 pages.

[ ] Send *The Traditional Text* hardback by Burgon ($16+$5
S&H) A hardback book, 384 pages in length.

[ ] Send *Causes of Corruption* by Burgon ($15+$5 S&H)
A hardback book, 360 pages in length.

[ ] Send *Inspiration and Interpretation*, Dean Burgon ($25+$5
S&H) A hardback book, 610 pages in length.

[ ] Send *Burgon's Warnings on Revision* by DAW ($7+$4
S&H) A perfect bound book, 120 pages in length.

] Send *Westcott & Hort's Greek Text & Theory Refuted by
Burgon's Revision Revised--Summarized* by Dr. D. A.
Waite ($7.00+$4 S&H), 120 pages, perfect bound.

[ ] Send *Dean Burgon's Confidence in KJB* by DAW ($3+$3)

[ ] Send *Vindicating Mark 16:9-20* by Dr. Waite ($3+$3 S&H)

[ ] Send *Summary of Traditional Text* by Dr. Waite ($3 +$3)

[ ] Send *Summary of Causes of Corruption*, DAW ($3+$3)

[ ] Send *Summary of Inspiration* by Dr. Waite ($3+$3 S&H)

Send or Call Orders to:
THE BIBLE FOR TODAY
900 Park Ave., Collingswood, NJ 08108
Phone: 856-854-4452; FAX:--2464; Orders: 1-800 JOHN 10:9

Order Blank (p. 5)

Name:_____

Address:_____

City & State:_____Zip:_____

Credit Card #:_____Expires:_____

Books by D. A. Waite, Jr.

[ ] Send *Readability of A.V. (KJB)* by D. A. Waite, Jr. ($6+$3)

[ ] Send *4,114 Definitions from the Defined King James Bible* by D. A. Waite, Jr. ($7.00+$4.00 S&H)

[ ] Send *The Doctored New Testament* by D. A. Waite, Jr. ($25+$5 S&H) Greek MSS differences shown, hardback

[ ] Send *Defined King James Bible* lg. prt. leather ($40+$7.50)

[ ] Send *Defined King James Bible* med. prt. leather ($35+$6)

Miscellaneous Authors

[ ] Send *Guide to Textual Criticism* by Edward Miller ($7+$4) Hardback book

[ ] Send *Scrivener's Greek New Testament Underlying the King James Bible*, hardback, ($14+$5 S&H)

[ ] Send *Scrivener's <u>Annotated</u> Greek New Testament*, by Dr. Frederick Scrivener: Hardback--($35+$5 S&H); Genuine Leather--($45+$5 S&H)

[ ] Send *Why Not the King James Bible?—An Answer to James White's KJVO Book* by Dr. K. D. DiVietro, $10+$5 S&H

[ ] Send Brochure #1: "*1000 Titles Defending KJB/TR*"(N.C.)

More Books by Dr. D. A. Waite

[ ] Send *Making Marriage Melodious* by Pastor D. A. Waite ($7+$4 S&H), perfect bound, 112 pages.

Send or Call Orders to:
THE BIBLE FOR TODAY
900 Park Ave., Collingswood, NJ 08108
Phone: 856-854-4452; FAX:--2464; Orders: 1-800 JOHN 10:9
E-Mail Orders: BFT@BibleForToday.org; Credit Cards OK

www.ingramcontent.com/pod-product-compliance
Lightning Source LLC
Chambersburg PA
CBHW071116090426
42737CB00013B/2601